The Intersection
of Race and Gender
in National Politics

The Intersection
of Race and Gender
in National Politics

Wanda V. Parham-Payne

LEXINGTON BOOKS
Lanham • Boulder • New York • London

Published by Lexington Books
An imprint of The Rowman & Littlefield Publishing Group, Inc.
4501 Forbes Boulevard, Suite 200, Lanham, Maryland 20706
www.rowman.com

Unit A, Whitacre Mews, 26-34 Stannary Street, London SE11 4AB

British Library Cataloguing in Publication Information Available

Library of Congress Cataloging-in-Publication Data Available

ISBN: 978-1-4985-1304-3 (cloth : alk. paper)
ISBN: 978-1-4985-1305-0 (electronic)

♾™ The paper used in this publication meets the minimum requirements of American
National Standard for Information Sciences—Permanence of Paper for Printed Library
Materials, ANSI/NISO Z39.48-1992.

Printed in the United States of America

This book is dedicated to the memories of my late mother June Edmonds Parham and my late grandparents Mary Catherine Edmonds, Christina Parham, and Horace Bolling Parham, Sr.

Contents

Acknowledgments

The completion of this book would not have been possible without the support and understanding of my husband, Rodney W. Payne, Jr., who read drafts and listened to me ruminate aloud. Hugs and appreciation to my family—Rodney Payne, III, Thomas A. Edmonds, Sr., Donna Wilson, Dwight Wilson, Jasmine and Jessica Wilson, Gabriella Payne, Ronald P. Parham, Sr., Candace Parham, Marjorie Gross, and Rodney Payne, Sr. Many thanks to my mentors, Drs. Bette J. Dickerson (American University) and Ralph C. Gomes (Howard University), who have given me timeless and invaluable guidance and advice. Additional gratitude is extended to my colleagues and friends including Dr. Janeula Burt, Dr. Nicole Branch, Dr. Vernese Edghill-Walden, Dr. Tekisha D. Everette, LaVoncye Mallory, and Dr. Nicole Rousseau for their encouragement and support. Finally, a special note of thanks is given to those women, standing at the intersection of race and gender, who offered their experiences and perceptions as black women in a society that is not always appreciative of their contributions and efforts. I appreciate your willingness in allowing me to capture your voices and share with others.

Chapter 1

Black Women's Politics

Historically Innate

A MATTER OF NECESSITY

Traditionally, the definition of politics pertains specifically to the administration of government. It may also relate to the development of policy that significantly influences and guides the manner in which persons residing under the purview of the policy live on a day-to-day basis. For this reason, politics often play an integral role in the lives of the general citizenry—both indirectly and directly. In fact, the inception of the United States was predicated on the creation of a government that encouraged freedom, as it was deemed necessary to a positive, high quality of life for all citizens. Some of the more memorable moments of this country's infancy entailed politically dramatic quests and protests that asserted the principles of democracy.

Despite the acknowledgment of unalienable rights for all citizens by the founding fathers, those representing various segments of the United States' population have been, and continue to be, marginalized, or to some degree, even excluded from influential roles within the government. In doing so, those persons who have been limited from influencing policy within government have had to rely on other means or methods to give voice to the respective issues most pertinent to them. As such, many of those who have been historically marginalized have been virtually compelled to act as agents of change—individually and collectively. For many, social activism has been the primary method for influencing political action to better the quality of lives for themselves, their families, and their communities. During the earlier days of the feminist movement, it was stressed that "the personal is political" in order to elucidate how women's daily, lived experience is greatly impacted by politics and is necessarily political (hooks, 2000: 26). Consequently, women were encouraged to give voice to their collective experience via social activism in order to facilitate political action.

However, according to Kimberle Crenshaw, mainstream feminism and feminist theory failed to comprehensively examine the lived experiences of all women, as it did not include an analysis of race in the context of gender. Thus, Crenshaw contended that social constructs such as race, gender, class, and so on are not individually existing oppressive forces. Instead, the aforementioned social constructs are oppressive forces that intersect and work as reciprocating and overlapping systems of power that impact the lived experiences of those who exist within these systems to varying degrees depending on their perceived location within the socially manufactured hierarchy (2000). Therefore, while women have had to contend with sexism and gender discrimination in many forms, black women have often had to cope with and/or resist the combined, or multiplicative, oppressive realities of gender and race.

A range of inequalities and discriminatory actions, including enslavement and the commodification of their reproductive labor, have left an indelible mark on the collective, lived experience of black women since their arrival in the United States. Like Crenshaw, in *Black Feminist Thought*, Collins places black women at the center of its analysis and illustrates that slavery remains the origin of black women's oppression (Hill-Collins 2000). Specifically, Collins argues that the role of black women during slavery shaped the societal images and expected subservient roles of black women for subsequent decades. Collins further delineates that such images and roles associated with black women are manifestations of the socially constructed Matrix of Domination that exists within and throughout society. According to Collins, the Matrix of Domination faced by black women is a multilayered mechanism produced to oppress individuals based on their race, social class, gender, sexuality, citizenship status, ethnicity, or age (2000). It is a hierarchical power relationship utilized in various political, social, and economic arenas (Hill-Collins 2000).

Although Collins acknowledges that the Matrix of Domination impacts all women, she avers that black women are especially impacted by the Matrix of Domination due to the simultaneous oppression of gender and race discrimination. Additionally, as Collins notes that black women experience oppression in varying degrees, she accordingly notes that the Matrix of Domination consequently impacts black women as dictated by their respective, individual experiences. To resist the varying degrees of oppression imposed by the Matrix of Domination, Collins contends that women should utilize their individual experiences to resist oppression and omission, which she contends, will ultimately result in individual and collective empowerment.

THE VARYING FORMS OF SOCIAL
AND POLITICAL ACTIVISM

One could assert that to be black and female is to be innately political, as the collective, lived experience of black women has often required that they act as advocates for themselves and their respective communities. Thus, as previously noted, because black women in the United States have frequently witnessed or found themselves on the receiving end of discriminatory actions grounded in sexism and/or racism, challenging the oppressive or harmful actions have naturally become part of the norm. Accordingly, an oppositional stance that rejects the hegemonic sexist and/or racist structure within the United States is often reflected, for instance, in the cultural production of those black women who are artists (e.g., lyrics, images, storylines, etc.).

In particular, early musical artists often performed songs that contained lyrics highlighting the plight of African-Americans in the United States (Feldstein 2013). In her song, "Strange Fruit," the legendary Billy Holiday brought attention to the frequent lynching of black persons in the South. As it contained lyrics referencing "bulging eyes and twisted mouths," "Strange Fruit" ultimately became a well-known political and social activist song. Similarly, the equally legendary Lena Horne released the song "Now" in 1963. In the song, Ms. Horne decries racial inequality and asserts that all persons are equal regardless of their race.

Like musical artists, black female literary writers and poets have also used their work to bring attention to inequality in America. Black female poets and literary writers of the twentieth and twenty-first centuries including, Toni Morrison and Sonia Sanchez, have used poetry as a mechanism for social activism and political action. Of the more widely cited poems, Maya Angelou's *Still I Rise* speaks of the resilience of African-Americans in which she notes, "Bringing the gifts that my ancestors gave, I am the dream and the hope of the slave" (Angelou 1994). Nikki Giovanni, now a distinguished university professor of English at Virginia Polytechnic Institute, also utilized poetry to highlight the historical lived experiences of black Americans. In her poem "Lorraine Hansberry: An Emotional View," Giovanni writes,

Time . . . to the Black American . . . has always been . . . a burden . . . from 1619 to now . . . we have played out our drama . . . before a reluctant time . . . No people on Earth . . . in all her history . . . has ever produced so many people . . . so generally considered "ahead of their time" . . . From the revolts in Africa . . . to our kidnapping . . . to the martyrs of freedom today . . . our people have been burdened . . . by someone else's sense . . . of the appropriate . . . Little Linda Brown was told . . . her school would be desegregated . . . "with all deliberate speed" and twenty-five years later . . . this is still . . . untrue . . . (pp. 242–43)[1]

In the same poem, Giovanni continued to observe,

I wish the battleships . . . had sailed down the Mississippi River . . . when Emmett Till was lynched . . . at the same speed they sped to Cuba . . . during the missile crisis. I wish food . . . had been airlifted . . . to the sharecroppers in Tennessee . . . when they were pushed off the land . . . for exercising the right to vote. (pp. 242–43)

Likewise, literary authors such as Lorraine Hansberry and Alice Walker often wrote stories such as "A Raisin in the Sun" and "The Color Purple" respectively that depicted the conditions under which black Americans have often had to exist while trying to maintain a sense of dignity, and thus, reaffirm their humanity. The aforementioned stories remain popular, via movies and stage plays, due to their illustration of the collective and historical experience of black Americans. The use of cinematic mediums to convey issues pertaining to the black community continues, as documentary filmmakers have furthered the tradition of displaying the social, economic, and political realities of black Americans. Although many documentary filmmakers are men, black women have created notable media pieces to visualize the issues that continue to impact black Americans, and Americans overall. For instance, Madeline Anderson and Portia Cobb have utilized cinematic tools to shed light on race and/or gender discrimination in award-winning documentaries. Such efforts continue the tradition of utilizing the arts as a tool of social and political activism among black women (Gateward 1999).

EARLY POLITICAL ACTIVISM

In addition to oppositional action through cultural production, black women have conscientiously engaged in organized efforts to shed light on the oppressive, and as previously noted, physically injurious conditions of African-Americans within the United States. Whenever possible, they also actively participated in the struggle for women's suffrage. Employing their available resources, skills, abilities, and/or professional occupations, black women have traditionally worked to ameliorate, and even eliminate, the social and economic disadvantages faced by marginalized groups and communities through strategic organizing. Thus, black women have historically demonstrated the propensity for wide-scale social betterment.

Notably, enslaved African women who escaped to freedom collaborated in the planning of revolts to assist other slaves in escaping to freedom. They also designed more covert networks such as the Underground Railroad in order to help other slaves escape to freedom without the confrontation innate to the slave revolts. Other free black women worked within antislavery organizations to bring about the abolition of slavery (Prestage 1991). Harriet Tubman, one of the most popular abolitionists during the slavery era, proved to be an invaluable strategist in the physical liberation of hundreds of slaves. Using the same skills she applied as a conductor on the Underground Railroad, Ms. Tubman also proved to be instrumental in the Union Army's efforts to defeat the Confederate Army. Ms. Tubman organized networks of black men who served as spies in the South. Indeed, utilizing intelligence gathered from her networks of spies, Ms. Tubman helped to lead one of the more successful military raids of the United States Civil War that simultaneously resulted in the freeing of approximately 700 slaves (Clinton 2005). One of the earliest feminists, Isabella Baumfree, better known as Sojourner Truth, was also an escaped slave and abolitionist who dedicated her life to human rights advocacy, and women's rights in particular. Although not formally educated, Ms. Truth nonetheless voiced the principles of democracy in her oratory and contended that women's suffrage was essential to the perpetuity of a self-professed egalitarian society. During her now widely read speech at the Women's Rights Conference in Akron, Ohio, later titled *Ain't I a Woman*, Ms. Truth insisted that women were integral members of society and therefore should be granted voting rights (Truth 1997). In sharing her thoughts on women's suffrage with those in attendance, Ms. Truth also gave voice to her experience as an enslaved woman, consequently illustrating the emotionally and physically excruciating experiences of enslaved black women.

POST-SLAVERY ACTIVISM

Upon the abolition of slavery, multiple political organizations were established with the distinct purpose of giving voice to marginalized populations and to facilitate civic engagement among those historically disenfranchised. Although black men were granted the right to vote with the Fifteenth Amendment to the United States Constitution, black women were not afforded the same rights as women, regardless of color, and would not be granted the right to vote until the ratification of the Nineteenth Amendment. Thus, women's suffragist organizations, for example, were created to aid women in obtaining the right to vote. However, although black women, such as Mary Church Terrell, an activist who sought to mitigate inequalities experienced by women and persons of color, willingly and enthusiastically joined what they initially perceived to be inclusive suffragist groups, they commonly encountered racialized opposition by white women within the organizations (Terrell 2005). Pointedly, white women within suffragist groups contended that the right to vote should not be extended to woman of color as well.

Due to such opposition, organizations such as the National Council of Negro Women (NCNW) were established for the purposes of bringing attention to the political, social, and economic issues faced by women *and* communities of color. The efforts and actions of the organizations, and persons associated with such organizations, have had and continue to have a significant impact on public policy.

Since its founding, for example, the NCNW has effectively collaborated with other civil and human rights organizations to promote and manifest positive social change. Dr. Mary McCleod Bethune, the visionary and former president of the NCNW, believed that establishing the NCNW would be a crucial step in aiding black women to move into national politics in order to address issues faced by socially and economically disadvantaged persons and groups (Hanson 2003). As evidenced in her address to the United States Congress, Dr. Bethune was astute in detailing how she foresaw the progress of minorities within the United States (Terrell 2005). She, like other politically savvy black women of her time, earnestly believed that education was critical to helping African-Americans overcome the issues prevalent in their respective communities. Precisely, Dr. Bethune, was dedicated to the education and training of black girls to assume leadership roles in order to advance the political, social, and economic conditions of the black community in general. Accordingly, prior to founding the NCNW, Dr. McLeod Bethune, also financed the erection of what is now Bethune-Cookman University which now offers four-year and graduate degrees to both men and women.

Along with other black women, Dr. Bethune increasingly became involved in national politics to bring attention to those matters exclusive to minorities. During the Coolidge, Hoover, and Roosevelt administrations, Dr. Bethune was a respected and effectual leader, deliberately expanding the number of black leaders within the national government, and ultimately, the allocation of social and economic programmatic resources for minority citizens.

Many other black women also inserted themselves into the national political spotlight challenging the treatment of minorities. In addition to multiple feminist organizations, Ida B. Wells was a founding member of the National Association for the Advancement for Colored People (NAACP). Since its founding in 1909, the NAACP continues to influence public policy by challenging systemic racial and economic discrimination in various sectors of society. Her role in the establishment of the NAACP coincides with her advocacy of black men, women, and children who often faced social problems including dilapidated segregated schools and widespread public lynchings (Bay 2010). As a newspaper owner, Ms. Wells, employed her talents and knowledge as a journalist and sociologist to launch a national crusade against lynching and implored then President William McKinley to take executive action. Her lobbying garnered overwhelming support and resulted in the recognition of lynching as a punishable crime. As well as effectively urging President William McKinley to take action against the lynching of blacks, Ms. Wells was concerned with gender-based discrimination. As such, she worked with the National Equal Rights League to address the subject to then President Woodrow Wilson in the hopes of ending gender-related employment discrimination (Bay 2010).

Between the years of 1908 and 1922, four historically black sororities were founded by African-American college women compelled to respond to the challenges unique to a time period rife with political and social tension and struggle (Ross 2001). Notably, they were active in facilitating access to the democratic process among previously disenfranchised southerners by launching voter registration drives and other civically minded efforts. For this reason, each sorority has embedded within its organizational history, a tradition of civic engagement. Hence, each sorority maintains programs or initiatives that seek to diminish, and ultimately eradicate, inequalities disproportionately impacting women, minorities, and low-income families (e.g., leadership academies, scholarships, public health initiatives, etc.). Consequently, despite their accomplishments as individual organizations, service to humanity and the struggle for political, social, and economic equality continues to be a shared imperative. Therefore, each of the four sororities continues to attract college educated women who desire to serve as leaders and effect social change within the global community overall, and within their respective, local communities, in particular.

The Civil Rights Movement was a collectively decisive response to the conditions of African-Americans in the south. The end of the Reconstruction Era introduced an assortment of obstacles. While the Fifteenth Amendment had granted the right to vote to African-American men, their right to vote was being challenged by carefully devised legal tactics (Branch 1988). Legal disenfranchisement was accompanied by de jure segregation in just about every sector of society. The ubiquitously brutal and disparate realities of segregation and disenfranchisement galvanized many to confront the oppressive systems and laws.

Often times, the Civil Rights Movement is often associated with the more popular names of Dr. Martin Luther King, Jr., Malcom X, Medgar Evers, and Marcus Garvey. Despite the popular perceptions of the Civil Rights Movement being a male-dominated era, women proved to be integral to sustaining the momentum needed to effect positive social change. Multiple organizations such as the Student Nonviolent Coordinating Committee (SNCC) relied heavily on the mental and physical labor of black women who were intricately involved in the planning and implementation of activities and campaigns on behalf of the organization. Initially conceived and subsequently founded by Ella Baker, SNCC conducted voter registration drives in socially and politically precarious locations throughout the south. Like the men within the organization, the women also participated in sit-ins resulting in their frequent arrests (Anderson-Bricker). Risking their lives, the women of SNCC participated in the creation and administration of Freedom Schools in largely segregated towns in order to educate, and ultimately empower, residents to engage in the democratic process and the overall struggle for political freedom. Simply stated, the work of black women inside and outside of organizations such as SNCC resulted in record numbers of southern and previously disenfranchised citizens becoming registered voters and participants in the democratic process.

PRESENT DAY

The Civil Rights Movement paved the way for many black women to enter the national political spotlight in primarily two ways. First, as widely acknowledged, the Voting Rights Act of 1965 was a manifestation of the Civil Rights Movement, effectively enfranchising numerous black voters and sparking an exponential increase in black voter participation. Secondly, as a result of their work as project directors, field secretaries, and political organizers, many black women gained the experience and credibility that made them optimal candidates for positions as legislators in their respective states and/or nationally. The convergence of increased black voter participation along with viable black female candidates produced a noticeable surge in the number of black women being elected to public office (Darcy and Hadley 1987). Individuals such as now United States Congressional Representatives Eleanor Holmes Norton, Maxine Waters, and Yvonne Brathwaite Burke were among the elected persons and have become political mainstays on the national stage. Others such as Dr. Joyce Ladner and Diane Nash also continued into successful careers as leaders within the realms of public service.

Yet, aside from the historical contributions of black women to the edification of the United States and the surge witnessed shortly after the passage of the Voting Rights of 1965, the number of women and black women in particular, within the national political sphere has remained sparse. The country recently hailed the vast increase in the number of women serving within both houses of the 113th United States Congress, but the number of black women elected to the United States Senate remained the same as it had for the prior 15 years—zero (Congressional Office of History and Preservation 2014). It was only recently that Dr. Condoleezza Rice was the first woman to serve as National Security Advisor. Likewise, she was also the first black woman to serve as United States Secretary of State. Still, while the twenty-first century witnessed the first Hispanic woman appointed to the United States

Supreme Court, not one black woman was even nominated nor presented for consideration. Equally pause worthy, no black woman has been supported in earnest contention for the United States Presidency or Vice Presidency. Shirley Chisolm, the first black woman elected to the United States Congress as a member of the House of Representatives, made an attempt to gain the nomination of her political party in her bid for the United States Presidency. Due to issues of race and sexism internal and external to the black community, Ms. Chisolm failed to garner significant voter and financial support from members of her political party (Chisolm 2010).

At present, Barack H. Obama II, the first African-American male to do so, is serving as the United States President. He was able to secure the nomination after defeating then former U.S. Senator Hillary Clinton, a white woman, who had galvanized thousands of supporters in her bid, including many women of all races. The campaigns of the two political contenders brought to light for the first time the issues of race and gender in the context of national politics. For many, it also brought to light the intersection of race and gender, and thus, the political perceptions and behaviors of black women voters in the political arena. Others also considered the political realities for black women politicians in the national setting. To be candid, some began to ponder if the historical campaigns of then United States Senator Barack Obama and then former United States Senator Hillary Clinton would somehow facilitate the major party nomination of a black woman in pursuit of the United States Presidency?

This question is becoming progressively more salient as the United States is rapidly changing in terms of demographics. Recent statistics released by the United States Census Bureau revealed for the first time ever, the majority of babies born were racial or ethnic minorities. This change in demographic trend supports hypotheses that, espouse overtime, the United States will indeed become a majority-minority country. Accordingly, the political landscape, including the political leaders, will be expected to transform to mirror the population. Not to mention, political leaders will have to amend their respective political agendas to adhere to the needs of the changing population.

Chiefly, shortly after the election of President Obama to the U.S. Presidency, many in the news media asserted that the United States had suddenly been ushered into a post-racial era. However, events that are converse to the notion of a post-racial nation have since occurred. The unprecedented social media campaign that took place after the murder of Trayvon Martin, and later Jordan Davis, exposed the raw emotion felt by many in response to the injuries racism continues to inflict. In the activist tradition of black women and in spite of coping with the loss of their children under tragic circumstances, the mothers of Trayvon Martin and Jordan Davis have opted to work as advocates and dismantle the laws that are widely perceived to have justified the killings of unarmed black teenagers.

In addition to equal pay, political and social issues such as the aforementioned persist in pervading the public discourse. As history has illustrated that women, and black women predominantly, have traditionally been the political forces to address concerns relevant to historically marginalized populations, it is only fitting that the presence of women of color on the national stage becomes more relevant. Recent rulings by the United States Supreme Court in reference to the Voting Rights Act, nevertheless, bear questions as to the potential impact of such on the election of women of color to public offices within the national sphere. Ultimately, the converging impacts of the election of the first African-American president, the historical primary campaign of Hillary Clinton, the transforming demographics of the United States, and modifications to the Voting Rights Act necessitate an analysis in the context of the political traditions and aspirations of black women.

NOTE

1. Excerpt from "Lorraine Hansberry," reprinted complete: "Time . . . right to vote." From *Those Who Ride the Night Winds* by Nikki Giovanni. Copyright 1983 by Nikki Giovanni. Reprinted by permission of HarperCollins Publishers.

Chapter 2

Policy Interests and Women, Minorities, and Minority Women

As discussed previously, women and racial and ethnic minorities have experienced absolute disenfranchisement in the past, and to some degree, continue to experience challenges regarding enfranchisement within the U.S. democracy. Their sparse representation in policy and legislative creating bodies has muffled their voices in the range of political discourses that ultimately shape the policies and legislations that govern American society. As a result, women and racial and ethnic minorities have experienced marginalization and/or unequal treatment in various social, political, and economic spheres. Needless to say, the unequal treatment of women and racial and ethnic minorities has, without a doubt, introduced social tensions and conflict on almost every level of society including, but not limited to, college campuses, healthcare delivery, the criminal justice system, and the workplace. Despite the advances that have been made in terms of gender equality and race relations, more progress remains to be achieved. More importantly, the needed progress is acutely grabbing the attention of members of the general citizenry who, once again, are increasing in diversity and, in some respects, social mobility.

In view of that, women and racial and ethnic minorities continue to have a keen interest in ensuring that their voices are heard in the political discourse (Pearson 2010). One of the more obvious ways to accomplish the inclusion of their voices has been the support and election of those who share similar demographic characteristics. In turn, the demographic make-up of elected officials, including nationally elected officials specifically, is of great interest to political and social scientists, scholars, and members of the general citizenry. Politicians' descriptive representation, commonly referring to their race, gender, geographic origin, in relation to their substantive representation, or willingness to advocate for particular groups, have been studied by political and social scientists in-depth (Tien and Levy 2008; O'rey et al.

2006; Swers 2001). Specifically, social and political scientists have probed and debated whether descriptive representation translates into substantive representation for those groups descriptively represented by political officials (Celis 2012; MacDonald and O'Brien 2011; Pearson and Dancy 2011; Baker and Cook 2005; Swers 2001; Barrett 1995). One or two political scholars have contended that descriptive representation does not result in substantive representation (Mansbridge 1999). Other political scholars have contended the opposite, demonstrating that descriptive representation heavily influences the substantive representation of a political official (MacDonald and O'Brien 2011; O'rey et al. 2006; Baker and Cook 2005; Thomas 2002; Barrett 1995). The logical assumption being that one's lived experience, as influenced by social characteristics such as gender, race, or ethnicity enables a first-hand, nuanced perspective of political and social issues or events through the lenses of those who share the same social characteristics (Tien and Levy 2008; Thomas 2002; Swers 2001; Barrett 1995). Further, the potentially shared lived experiences of those belonging to historically marginalized groups possess an empathy that enables them to give voice to concerns or issues specific to such communities (Baker and Cook 2005; Barrett 1995).

The following discussion delves into the role women legislators, minority legislators, and women legislators of color have played and continue to play in the introduction and support of issues that impact the everyday lives of women, people of color, and their families.

WOMEN

As the electorate evolves in terms of its diversity, out of pure necessity, the policies that impact it are sure to do so as well. In 2012, close to 40 percent of women, regardless of generation, were in possession of a college degree (Bureau of Labor Statistics 2014). More so, the growing presence of Generation X and Millennial women, who are matriculating toward postsecondary degrees at a far greater rate than previous generations, mandates the creation of policies that are congruent with the changing social and economic behaviors of women. This increase in education has naturally enabled more women to enter into professional occupations. According to the Bureau of Labor Statistics (BLS), women make up slightly more than half (52 percent) of the professional and managerial workforce (BLS 2014). The greater educational attainment of women in recent decades has, as one would expect, spurred greater earning power among women as well. Whereas women once earned, on average, a little more than half of what men earned, their average earnings have improved (BLS 2014). (Of course, as discussed later in this chapter, there is definitely room for improvement.) Hence, as opposed to several decades ago, women are more independent and less willing to feel dependent upon a man for financial security. The greater proportion of divorced women than married women engaged in the paid labor force may be attributable to this earnings trend (BLS 2014). Moreover, although many divorced women may work out of necessity, their earning power may also serve as a source of financial independence allowing them to serve as heads of households. An almost ubiquitous acceptance of divorce and out-of-wedlock births within American society has, to some degree, served as an impetus for women's willingness to consider and/or pursue family formation outside of what was once the traditional norm (Parham-Payne, Dickerson, and Everette 2013; Dickerson, Parham-Payne, and Everette 2012). This has arguably resulted in an exponential increase in number of single, female-headed households (Parham-Payne, Dickerson, and Everette 2013).

Changes in women's workforce participation and family formation, in part, have required women to become political stakeholders in order to ensure that their voices are heard, and more tangibly, their social, economic, and political needs are met. Women comprise a huge venerable voting block helping both male and female candidates to obtain their respective sought after offices (Carroll and Fox 2014). Though not proportionate to their actual numbers within the U.S. citizenry, the number of women occupying political offices is more now than ever.

Because of the increasing political power of women, descriptive versus substantive representation in the context of gender has been of particular interest to political and social scholars. In particular, political, social, and gender scholars have pondered whether female politicians are more likely than male politicians to advance the issues most relevant to the female citizenry (MacDonald and O'Brien 2011; Thomas 2002; Swers 2001). In doing so, a few have speculated if women legislators are as effective as male legislators (Jeydal and Taylor 2003). Empirical evidence has determined that, although the leadership style of women legislators has proven to be more collaborative than men's resulting in greater productivity policy wise, there remain challenges for women legislators (Volden, Wisemen, and Wittmer 2010; Jeydal and Taylor 2003). One of the significant challenges faced by female legislators is often that of seniority. Congressional members with greater seniority lead committees and occupy seats on more impacting and actionable committees (Jeydal and Taylor 2003). For example, in the national legislative body, women legislators are woefully outnumbered; typically have fewer terms under their belts making them more junior in terms of committee assignments and roles.

Nonetheless, they are in fact just as, if not more, active as their male counterparts. Analyses of U.S. Congressional floor speeches focusing on a range of topics, have proven that Democratic and Republican women tend to give more floor speeches than men (Pearson and Dancy 2011; Shogan 2001). Still, studies have determined that women legislators were more likely than their male counterparts to engage in debates on those issues that are typically labeled as "liberal" and "feminist" including family and social welfare-oriented issues such as healthcare and education (Volden, Wiseman, and Wittmer 2013; Swers 2001; Thomas 1997). For instance, Pearson and Dancy found that women federal legislators were more likely to engage in debates pertaining to the Family Medical and Leave Act (FMLA) (2011). Upon conducting an analysis of state legislators' level of support for state welfare legislation, Poggione determined that women state legislators exhibited more liberal ideologies, and therefore, were more supportive of government policies that fund and provide access to job counseling and social services for at-risk children (2004).

In 2001, it was concluded that the proportion of women in Congressional leadership roles impacts the formulation of policies specific to women's health (Tolbert and Steuernagel). Activities of recent Congresses have reflected such. As women continue to increase in number within the federal legislative body especially, greater attention has been paid to women's health issues. The Office of Legislative Policy and Analysis (OLPA) at the National Institutes of Health (NIH) documented the introduction of over 50 bills during the 108th Congress related specifically to women's health issues. Bills introduced targeted various diseases and conditions that have disproportionate or prejudicial impact on women including breast cancer, diabetes, heart disease, scleroderma, and so on. Subsequent Congresses realized the same level of focus on women's health issues. The 113th Congress had multiple accomplishments regarding women's health issues including the reauthorization of the Early Awareness Requires Learning Young (EARLY) Act and the passage of a resolution declaring September 2013 as Ovarian Cancer Awareness Month.

Reproductive Rights

According to the Kaiser Family Foundation, a nationally representative survey of over 1,000 respondents concluded that close to 40 percent of those interviewed stated that reproductive rights should be a high priority for the 113th Congress. Therefore, it is of no surprise that the topic of reproductive rights remains a topic germane to women voters. As discussed later in Chapter 5, women's political action committees such as EMILY's List usually promote Democratic female candidates who are committed to advocating for reproductive rights, and more explicitly, a women's right to choose in the areas of family planning and formation.

The salience of reproductive rights continues to be reinforced via Congressional actions such as committee and floor debates that continue to take place despite the *Roe v. Wade* decision over 40 years ago. In 2012, for instance, there were criticisms of the mandate that employee health plans cover birth control per the Affordable Care Act (ACA). Employers with religious affiliations openly questioned whether the ACA's birth control coverage mandate violated religious freedoms. To debate the issue, House Representative Darryl Issa (CA), convened a panel of predominantly male speakers representing various employers with religious affiliations. The make-up of the panel received backlash from female members of the House as well as social media users who were watching the panel unfold on television (Flock 2012). Members of the media expressed that the committee silenced or failed to acknowledge the very population whose reproductive rights were being discussed (Zornick 2012; Flock 2012; Miller 2012). Possessing a point of view different from their male peers, women legislators have historically advocated for women's reproductive rights, and therefore, are more likely to vote in favor of women's reproductive rights (Norton 1999). The omission of women from the above referenced birth control discussion prevented a balanced and comprehensive exchange of views, and consequently, was a monumental oversight to say the least.

Falling under the realm of reproductive rights is the right to legally access an abortion. In 1973, as a result of *Roe v. Wade*, the U.S. Supreme Court decided that a woman has a legal right to terminate a pregnancy during the first 12 weeks of gestation in a manner that is safe to her. Since then, there have been innumerable criticisms of and challenges to the ruling on both the state and federal levels. The most effective challenges to the U.S. Supreme Court ruling have been through the creation and implementation of restrictions on the state level. In addition to several states de-funding Planned Parenthood in 2011, as of 2015, almost three-quarters of states have implemented laws requiring that abortions only be performed by a licensed physician (Boonstra and Nash 2014; Guttmacher Institute 2015). Admittedly, such a requirement seeks to ensure that the skills and expertise necessary in case of an emergency are readily available to ensure the well-being of the mother. However, other states have implemented laws that many abortion rights advocates believe place unnecessary emotional hardship on the mother. For instance, several states require that women receive counseling or written materials on ultrasound services prior to having an abortion. Three states mandate that a transvaginal ultrasound, an extremely intrusive procedure, be conducted prior to an abortion and that the resulting image be shown and described to the woman seeking an abortion (Guttmacher Institute 2015; Boonstra and Nash 2014). In another related example, in 2015, 26 states require that a woman seeking an abortion wait a minimum of 24 hours between counseling and the actual procedure (Guttmacher Institute 2015; Boonstra and Nash 2014). Joining Missouri, South Dakota, and Utah, the North Carolina state legislature most recently approved the institution of a 72-hour waiting period (Guttmacher 2015). Advancing the restrictive efforts of the states, in 2015, in a strategic move to undermine *Roe v. Wade*, conservative, Republican members of the U.S. House passed a bill indefinitely preventing the use of federal funding, by way of ACA subsidies, on abortions. It should be noted the bill was perceived to be a watered-down version of a previous piece of legislation that was much more restrictive in nature (Hee Lee 2015).

Equal Pay

Although women are participating in the paid labor force at unprecedented rates, they continue to face discrimination on the job in terms of promotion and equal pay. Male-dominated occupations, largely in the science and technology sectors, tend to be more lucrative. In addition, despite being integral to everyday, societal operations, female-dominated occupations pay less than those occupations dominated by their males (e.g., primary and secondary school teachers, social workers, etc.). Due to persisting traditional gender roles that frown on women taking on leadership positions, men are more likely to be promoted and occupy organizational leadership positions while women remain in lower-ranked, lower-paying positions. Not to mention, women remain largely responsible for home and family tasks. A study conducted by Lawless and Fox affirmed what has been suspected to be the case for many years (2012). Despite the educational and professional gains made by women in the last two generations, women remain primarily responsible for household chores and serving as the primary childcare provider. This includes households where both the man and woman hold professional occupations. Such responsibilities potentially obscure their ability to pursue career advancement opportunities.

As such, equal pay for women continues to gain mounting attention. Women continue to be paid less for performing the same jobs and accompanying duties as men. On average, women are paid 77 cents for every dollar a man is paid. Taking into consideration the rise of single, female-headed households in recent decades this has indelible impacts on children of such households. A lack of equal pay impedes a mother's ability to save adequately for college as well as provide comfortable and safe housing for their family. Ultimately, equal pay has an impact on the short-term and long-term security and stability of many female-headed households.

Most recently, the U.S. Senate voted down a bill that would have ensured equal pay for women. In order to pass, the bill needed 60 votes but fell short of the required number by merely eight votes. However, not one Republican voted in support of the bill including the four female GOP Senators who had previously voiced their support for the bill. Aside from the obvious partisan politics, the ongoing gender imbalance within the upper chamber of the Congress no doubt had an adverse impact on the outcome of the vote. Moreover, the demographic make-up of the Republican Senate, which is heavily and disproportionately male, potentially negates its ability to identify with and/or have empathy for those who earn less due to gender. Therefore, a critical mass of women may be needed in the upper chamber of the legislative body for the advancement of women's issues.

"Non-Women's" Issues

However, political, social, and gender scholars have noted that women are also more inclined to provide substantive representation on non-gender-specific issues. Bivariate analyses have revealed that Congresswomen also gave more than half of speeches during floor debates on issues pertaining to trade and defense. Thus, women legislators have demonstrated their competencies as leaders and policy creators on issues outside of what has traditionally been categorized as "women's issues" (Pearson and Dancey 2011). In a more prominent example of substantive representation on "non-women's issues," following the tragic events in Newtown, Connecticut that left over 20 students and teachers dead, U.S. Senator Dianne Feinstein (D-CA) proposed the reinstatement of the assault weapons ban that she played an integral role in passing in 1994. According to the Center for American Women and Politics at Rutgers University, 83 percent of female legislators in the lower house supported the assault weapons ban while only 50 percent of men in the lower house supported the ban when it was initially passed (Dittmar 2012). If reinstated, the legislation, which expired in 2004, would have re-established bans on high-capacity, military style weapons known to kill copious amounts of people in a short period of time. The bill to reinstate the ban was cosponsored by 23 Democratic Senators including seven women senators. The debate regarding gun control continues in the public discourse. As news outlets highlight mass shootings that are seemingly becoming more and more frequent, gun control will likely remain a subject of debate for federal and state legislators as well.

In an additional example, U.S. Senator Elizabeth Warren (D-MA), an ardent supporter of American consumers, who continues to speak out against predatory financial practices, has consistently supported bills that facilitate transparency and prevent economic exploitation. For example, she voted in support of the Credit Card Holders Bill of Rights Act of 2009 that mandated credit card companies amend their polices to be more transparent in nature in regard to due dates, interest, fees, and so on. It also placed restrictions on credit cards for minors. The bill, known as H.R. 627, was cosponsored by approximately 100 members of the U.S. House of Representatives. Among those cosponsoring the bill, 25 percent were women.

Thus, while the issues of gun control and financial security typically do not fall within the traditional domain of "women's issues," it does fall under the realm of general welfare or well-being—an area typically supported by the efforts of women legislators.

MINORITIES

Myriad studies have been conducted to explore a potentially existing relationship between political representatives' race and/or ethnic identity and substantive representation in government bodies. While a couple of studies found negligible evidence to support such a contention due to barriers such as seniority and committee membership type (Preuhs 2006; Jeydel and Taylor 2003), results from others studies have consistently revealed otherwise (Rocca, Sanchez, and Nikora 2009; Pinney and Serra 2002). Accordingly, in addition to being descriptively representative, legislators of color have proven to be substantively representative as well, utilizing their authority to craft and/or support policies that are in the interest of racial and ethnic minorities. In particular, Baker and Cook (2005) sought to determine if a link exists between descriptive and substantive African-American interest in the U.S. Congress. After looking at bill sponsorships and floor speeches of African-American Congressional representatives, study investigators found evidence to support a link between descriptive and substantive representation among African-American Congressional members. Subsequently, in 2011, after looking at data generated during the 105th to 108th Congresses, Preuhs and Hero concluded that African-American and Latino representatives were influenced by cues outside of the dichotomous liberal versus conservative model to which many non-minority representatives adhere.

Legislators of color have proven to be essential in the struggle for civil rights and addressing concerns expressly of interest to persons of color. For example, Tien and Levy determined that, upon conducting an analysis of U.S. House floor debates, African-Americans representatives have affected the manner in which white representatives engage in discussions surrounding civil rights (2008). Simply stated, the presence of racial and ethnic minorities has helped to transform and possibly modulate discussions specific to racial and ethnic minorities.

Although one's racial and/or ethnic identity may not serve as an automatic qualifier to represent a community or jurisdiction, too many, it often influences the lens through which societal operations and events are perceived. For those political representatives belonging to a historically marginalized group or community, there is an assumption that they too share a nuanced understanding of past and present concerns and interests of those also belonging to the group or community. As reflected above, minorities have and continue to serve as effective advocates and influences on issues of civil rights (Preuhs and Hero 2011). As the proportion of racial and ethnic minorities continues to account for the greater proportion of U.S. citizens and active voters, social and political issues specific to traditionally marginalized populations will remain salient. The following are select issues encountered by racial and ethnic minorities.

Health Disparities

Like women, racial and ethnic minorities contend with health-related issues specific to them. The Centers for Disease Control (CDC) releases results of ongoing disease surveillance activities annually. Each year, statistics illustrate that African-Americans and Hispanics are more likely to be diagnosed with chronic diseases such as diabetes, coronary heart disease, hypertension, and so on. On top of that, African-Americans and Hispanics are more likely to experience complications related to those diseases at a greater rate than their white counterparts. One of the primary contributors to the existing health disparities is a lack of health insurance among racial and ethnic minorities. A lack of health insurance prevents individuals from securing the preventative health care that often minimizes or stops complications from routine illnesses or injuries from increasing in severity (Lillie-Blanton and Hoffman 2005, Zuvekas and Taliaferro 2003; Weinberger, Oddone, and Henderson 1996). Furthermore, health insurance enables access to other health care services such as medication and patient education to properly manage acute and chronic illnesses.

Acknowledging the impact that a lack of health insurance has on select segments of the population including low-income and racial and ethnic minorities, members of Congress and President Obama enacted the Patient Protection and Affordable Care Act (ACA), colloquially known as "Obamacare." Initially, various members of Congress and President Obama sought to establish a public option as a step toward universal health care. His initial proposal met resistance by select members of Congress, however, and was pared down resulting in expanded health coverage for those who previously fell in the "gap"—those who make too much to qualify for Medicaid but not enough to afford private insurance (Parham-Payne and Saxton-Ross 2010). Accordingly, "Obamacare" provided for states' expansion of their respective Medicaid programs allowing low-income adults without children to apply without a waiver. Of course, it should be noted that not all states have opted to expand Medicaid. As of May 2015, 30 states have adopted Medicaid expansion and an additional three are contemplating expansion. The remaining has opted not to expand (Kaiser Family Foundation 2015). The ACA also created an insurance health exchange so that citizens can choose from a variety of private insurance plans based on their individual needs. In addition, the ACA mandates that employers with a certain number of employees provide health insurance coverage to those employees.

The ACA guarantees coverage regardless of pre-existing conditions to prevent citizens from being denied coverage or paying astronomical fees. This is especially a concern for racial and ethnic minorities who, as previously noted, experience high rates of chronic diseases due to a range of reasons pertaining to genetics and disparities in income and geographical structure and access (LaVeist et al. 2009; Airhihenbuwa et al. 2004; Pappas et al. 1997; Lillie-Blanton et al. 1996). The ACA was the first landmark healthcare legislation since Title XIX—the Social Security Act which established Medicare. It should be noted that the legislation was cosponsored by 40 members of the House of Representatives. Of the 40 cosponsors of the bill, close to one-quarter, or 22 percent to be exact, belonged to a racial or ethnic minority group.

Police Brutality and Black Lives Matter

Most prominently, the news has been inundated with news of racially incendiary events not seen since the 1960s. The shootings of unarmed black teenagers have galvanized a movement, Black Lives Matter, which does not appear to be short-lived. The movement was initially sparked by the killing of Trayvon Martin, who was shot and killed by neighborhood watchman George Zimmerman while returning home from a nearby convenience store. Zimmerman asserted that Martin looked suspicious because he was wearing a sweatshirt with a hood on while walking through the neighborhood. It was after several weeks of protests and public demands for his arrest and trial that he was in fact arrested. He was later found not guilty of Martin's murder per Florida's "Stand Your Ground" law. The death of Trayvon Martin was one of the more prominent controversies in recent years to stir up conversations and debates regarding the role of race in human interactions. It also highlighted racial disparities in "Stand Your Ground" laws nationwide (Roman 2013). In response to the Zimmerman verdict, members of the Congressional Black Caucus (CBC) called for repeals of "Stand Your Ground" laws nationwide, including in Florida where another teenager, Jordan Davis, was shot and killed during an altercation stemming from what a white male assailant termed as "loud music." Davis' murderer was convicted of all counts against him, except Davis' homicide.

It should go without saying that the aforementioned events shed light on the continued demonization of black men nationwide. This type of attention had not been seen for almost 20 years. In the 1990s, the issue of racial profiling was introduced to the forefront of the nation's conscience. High-profile beatings and shootings of unarmed men proved to be alarming to many in mainstream America (e.g., Rodney King, Amadou Diallo, etc.). Unfortunately, it was merely viewed as the status quo by many minorities. These violent attacks are often part of a larger problem popularly referred to as racial profiling. A study conducted on the New Jersey Turnpike revealed that an inordinately larger proportion of African-American and Hispanic males were stopped and/or arrested when compared to white males (Harris 1999). To many, it seems the issue of racial profiling, also referred to as "driving while black" by many in the African-American community, has become virtually a daily occurrence among many minority communities. Due to the reported extent of racial profiling, many African-American males take extraordinary precaution to avoid potentially fatal encounters with law enforcement officials. For example, focus groups conducted with African-Americans addressed the issue of racial profiling. One participant explained, "I would never stop for a police car until I am around other people who would be able to see me" (Birzee and Smith-Mahdi 2006).

An experimental study conducted by Peruche and Plant determined that white officers were more likely to shoot an unarmed African-American "suspect" than an unarmed white "suspect" (2006). When probed, study investigators discovered that white police officers who had positive experiences with African-Americans in their personal lives were less likely to shoot at unarmed African-American "suspects." Conversely, white police officers who had negative experiences with African-Americans in their personal lives were more likely to shoot at unarmed men of color (2006). Moreover, investigators observed that, when shown pictures of African-American men in a line-up fashion, police officers were more likely to choose those "suspects" that possessed stereotypical African-American features (e.g., wide nose, big lips, etc.) (Peruche and Plant 2006).

As a result, police-involved shootings resulting in the deaths of a disproportionate number of unarmed black men, women, and children continue in what has been termed a post-racial nation. Since the shooting death of unarmed teenager Trayvon Martin, the killings of teenagers of color have arrested the attention and conscience of many Americans. Although Trayvon's killer was not a police officer, his subsequent lack of conviction made many feel as if the judicial system was complicit in his death, undergirding seething emotions among communities color who were fed up with the trivialization of their humanity. Police-involved shootings of Rekia Boyd, Michael Brown, Ramarley Graham, and nine-year-old Aiyana Stanley-Jones shortly thereafter added fuel to a simmering flame of emotions once all of the police officers involved were either not indicted or found not guilty.

Not to mention, the events and contexts in which the aforementioned shootings continue to occur has awakened a moral outrage among many in and outside of communities of color. In April 2015, a bystander captured on video a white police officer unequivocally shoot an unarmed man, Walter Scott, in the back as he attempted to flee. In a subsequent event, another bystander captured an injured African-American man being placed into a police van by two police officers. The man, Freddie Gray, who could barely stand at the time of his arrest, later died of his injuries allegedly sustained while in police custody en route to the police station. Prior to the above police-involved events, on July 17, 2014, in Staten Island, New York, police officers approached Eric Garner for selling single, unpackaged cigarettes. As police officers tried to arrest him, they placed Mr. Garner in a chokehold, a maneuver banned by the New York City Police Department, resulting in the restriction of oxygen. Mr. Garner repeatedly told the police officers that he was unable to breathe, and they continued to restrain him. Minutes later, he lay motionless on the ground.

The events above are known because they too were captured on video by a bystander. Because of the video evidence, many were confident that the police officers would be indicted. However, this was not the case. Upon announcing that the police officers would not be indicted despite clear video evidence, protests erupted in New York City and in other major cities across the country. Due to advances in social media and increases in smart phone usage, nefarious encounters between police officers and minority members of society have been brought to light. Such events continue to remain in the spotlight, as online platforms such as YouTube, Facebook, and Twitter have opened up the conversation to the masses, and therefore, shaped the political impetus and policy implications of these incidents.

U.S. Senator Corey Booker (D-NJ), the sole African-American in the Senate, and U.S. Senator Barbara Boxer (D-CA) therefore proposed the Police Reporting of Information, Data and Evidence (P.RI.D.E.) Act. The legislation would require police departments to report the number and relevant details, including race, age, and gender of all involved persons, to the U.S. Department of Justice if enacted. Senators Booker and Boxer proposed P.R.I.D.E. subsequent to a newspaper article that illustrated the disproportionate number of persons of colors killed at the hands of police officers.

Unemployment

Despite increases in education attainment among racial and ethnic minorities, securing gainful employment at rates comparable to whites continues to be a challenge. While some have attributed the high rates of unemployment to a lack of professional networks, others have attributed the high rates to systemic discrimination among employers (Hardaway and McLoyd 2009; Ward and Ong 2006; Pager 2003). In a stunning demonstration of the unemployment discrimination faced by minorities, and minority males explicitly, Pager found that a well-qualified, educated African-American male is less likely to secure employment than a white male with a criminal record (2003). Pager's study provides insight into the ongoing disproportionate unemployment rates for African-Americans overall. Data analyses conducted by the Bureau of Labor Statistics (BLS) demonstrate that African-Americans at all education levels are more likely to be unemployed than their white counterparts (2010). Similarly, BLS data analyses demonstrate that African-Americans are the least likely to hold managerial or executive positions; positions that offer generous compensation (Bureau of Labor Statistics 2010). Therefore, it is not surprising that unemployment continues to be an issue for those African-American males residing in urban areas. In May 2011, the unemployment rate for African-American males peaked at 17.5 percent. Surprisingly, this was lower than unemployment rates for African-American males in 2010 when the rate was over 20 percent. Five years later, the rate has dramatically decreased to 9.2 percent. Yet, it is still more than twice the unemployment rate of white males ages 20 and over at 4.4 percent (Bureau of Labor Statistics 2015). Therefore, African-American males continue to have the highest unemployment rates than men in any other racial or ethnic group (Bureau of Labor Statistics 2015).

The actions of members of the CBC, Congressional Hispanic Caucus, and other federal legislators such as Senators Booker and Boxer reflect the literature regarding the relationship between descriptive representation and substantive representation. As members of historically marginalized communities and populations, legislators of color possess a personal, and therefore a naturally, nuanced understanding of the issues and challenges encountered by those belonging to racial and ethnic minority groups. Using this empathy, many have and continue to apply this particular understanding to the manner in which they approach their legislative activities. Although they remain in the minority and must consequently work collaboratively with their white counterparts, their presence in the federal legislative body has facilitated greater recognition of the social and economic conditions of racial and ethnic minorities within the United States.

MINORITY WOMEN

As members of the CBC and Congressional Women's Caucus, black women legislators have engaged in the policy efforts and legislative action pertaining to the aforementioned. However, they have also worked from a perspective possessed by only them. In keeping with their tradition as activists for the socially and economically disadvantaged, women of color in legislatures have often advocated for those policies that seek to improve or advance the conditions of those who have often been oppressed or restricted. Clawson and Clark (2003) contended that, because of black women's experiences with racism and sexism, they possess an inimitable perspective on those concerns or social problems that pertain to women and persons of color. Furthermore, Clawson and Clark determined that, for black women, race and gender exist on a single attitudinal dimension, as they are inextricably intertwined due to their simultaneous and reciprocating influence on their lived experiences. Because of this dual influence, black women in legislative bodies remain acutely aware of the policy needs of women and racial and ethnic minorities. More importantly, as individuals who straddle between being both female and persons of color, they have an intimate knowledge of what it means to belong to a marginalized group or community (O'rey et al. 2006).

Although the number of women serving in the U.S. Senate has increased, the number of women of color remains stagnant. Presently, the U.S. Senator from the State of Hawaii is the only woman of color serving in the upper house, and not since Carol Mosley-Braun has a woman of African descent served in the U.S. Senate. However, the diversity of women in the U.S. House of Representatives is greater though in no way proportionate or representative of the actual female U.S. electorate. In the face of their limited representation, like their white female and minority male counterparts, women of color in the U.S. House of Representatives substantively represent the interests of women and minority individuals and families equally and simultaneously. Furthermore, they develop and sponsor those bills or policies that serve multiple purposes in aiding the economic development and well-being of families. In as much, studies have discovered that black women have historically advocated for those policies that facilitate access to education, employment, healthcare, housing, and so on. (Barrett 1995). In a notable example, in 2013 U.S. Representative Gwen Moore (D-WI) introduced a bill to reauthorize and amend the Violence Against Women Act which incorporated language specific to American Indian women and immigrant women and children. In addition to a myriad of male representatives, the bill was cosponsored by female members of the Congressional Black Caucus and the Congressional Hispanic Caucus. As another example, Congresswoman Donna Edwards (D-MD), in conjunction with Congresswoman Shelley Capito (R-WV), introduced a resolution acknowledging the impact of heart disease on women. In documenting her support, she also acknowledged the disparate impact of heart disease on African-American women and the need for education among Latinas. Explicitly, she stated, "I am concerned that heart disease claims the lives of more than 400,000 women each year and almost half of all African-American women have some form of cardiovascular disease. Meanwhile, awareness among Latinas that heart disease is the leading cause of death remains at just 34 percent" (Edwards, nd).

MAKING THE CONNECTION

Smooth made a similar contention in her interviews with black female state legislatures (2011). Although the state legislatures interviewed by Smooth stated that they have a keen interest in supporting women's issues, she found that what the state legislatures identified as women's issues were actually broader in scale and cut across social and economic domains including child health and well-being (Smooth 2011). The revelations of state legislatures illustrated the multifaceted and complex nature of what are traditionally, and arguably narrowly, defined as women's issues and further reiterated black female legislatures' encompassing understanding of the interconnectedness of social issues impacting the larger society. Consequently, on the federal level, in addition to women's issues, women who stand at the intersection of race and gender manifest the findings of Smooth through their continued support and introduction of legislation and policies that seek to improve the social and economic conditions of middle-class families as well as those living in the margins of society.

As an example, Congresswoman Barbara Lee voiced her support for equal pay for women. In her statement of support, she noted the intersecting realities of race and gender as well as the impact of unequal pay on families. She observed,

> For every dollar a man earns, a woman earns just 78 cents. For women of color, the situation is even worse. On average, African-American women earn just 64 cents and Latinas earn a mere 56 cents for every dollar paid to white men . . . The wage gap not only hurts women; it hurts their families and the economy. It's kitchen table economics. When women are paid less, families have less money for every day essentials.[1] (Lee)

Without question, Congresswoman Lee's equal pay remarks note the apparent gender disparities experienced by women in the U.S. labor force. Her remarks also highlight the intersecting impact of race and gender on the incomes of women of color. Consequently, while a white man will earn $100,000, a black woman will only earn $64,000 for performing the same job function. Congresswoman Lee's remarks also went a step further in acknowledging the effects of disparate pay on the families of women and women of color. In doing so, she implicated the financial effects with which families, including those headed by single women and women of color, must contend.

On issues of the environment, Congresswoman Lee has also highlighted the disproportionate effect of climate change on the health and well-being of African-Americans, and African-American children especially. At a press conference on climate change, Congresswoman Lee was quoted as saying,

> For too long, we have overlooked the impact of environmental issues on minority communities in this country . . . We know that environmental decisions disproportionately affect African Americans and other people of color because it is in our communities, our homes, our places, where the worst environmental crises occur. Life expectancy itself is an environmental justice issue. In this country, life expectancy projections are shaped as much by race as by gender. These disparities follow a cradle to grave cycle; beginning with infant mortality, continuing with workplace hazards and increased exposure to pollution . . . Death rates from asthma and a host of other treatable diseases are also significantly higher among African Americans that any other ethnic group . . . In fact, children in West Oakland are seven times more likely to be hospitalized for asthma than children in the rest of California.

Firstly, Congresswoman Lee's reference to the cumulative effects of race and gender on life expectancy once again illustrates her views of environmental disparities as a dual-axis issue. Secondly, her reference to environmental disparities as a source of disease for people of color and children also reinforces the tradition of women legislators of color to advocate on behalf of communities historically relegated to the margins.

One of the longest serving women of color in the U.S. House of Representatives, Congresswoman Maxine Waters (D-CA) recently voted to support a bill to fund transportation infrastructure. In a recent statement published on her website, Waters explained that the funding of transportation served multiple purposes that ultimately have positive impacts on middle- and working-class families. A portion of her statement read,

> Federal investment in our nation's transportation system is essential. The American Society of Civil Engineers gave the public infrastructure of the United States a grade of "D+" in 2013 and estimated that we will need to invest $3.6 trillion by 2020 in order to improve the condition of our infrastructure . . . Rebuilding our nation's infrastructure creates jobs that are desperately needed throughout the country. The economy is still struggling to recover from the recession. The unemployment rate is 5.4 percent nationwide and is significantly higher in some minority and disadvantaged communities. Transportation funding is clearly good for the economy. (Waters)

Reading Representative Waters' statement it is quite apparent that her supportive efforts of transportation funding were to address the potential safety issues associated with an infrastructure that has been determined to be inadequate. She further linked the need for transportation funding to the recovering economy and resulting unemployment rate. Even more so, she addressed the economic conditions of marginal and predominantly minority communities and detailed the impact the legislation could potentially have on such communities.

Comparably, in detailing her support for affordable and accessible child care, Congresswoman Donna Edwards (D-MD), a demonstrated supporter of women's rights and Chair of the Democratic Women's Working Group, observed the connection between and among affordable child care, financial stability, worker productivity, and sustaining the U.S. labor force. She expounded,

> Working families benefit greatly from child care, but rising costs have limited their access. According to a report by Child Care Aware, worker absenteeism as a result of disruptions in child care costs United States businesses $3 billion annually. Giving working parents safe and reliable child care brings peace of mind and stability to families, which increases productivity and maintains our country's competitive workforce. (Edwards)

Congresswoman Edwards' observations regarding child care costs and the economy are especially pertinent topics for women who are more likely to be the caregivers within the family structure. However, Edwards, reflecting Smooth's findings, explained how childcare, and childcare costs especially, can serve as an impediment to families and productivity among the overall American workforce. Congresswoman Edwards' comments logically revealed an interconnectedness of the issues and expressed that, what was once labeled a woman's issue, is in fact a gender neutral issue that has ripple effects on the economy.

The above examples are a small proportion of the policy stances and advocacy efforts that women of color within the national legislative body have respectively taken or made. In the end, women of color in the federal legislative body are active on a range of issues—not just those traditionally viewed as "women's issues." However, on "women's" health issues for example, they are also inclined to advocate on behalf of women of color who are usually disproportionately affected by infirmities such as heart disease or breast cancer. Still, because of their experiences as both women and racial and/or ethnic minorities, they possess a more comprehensive perception or diverse interpretation of issues facing the American public. On "non-women's" issues such as the environment and transportation, they lend a unique perspective to the political discourse from their experiences as dual minorities often representing racially and/or ethnically diverse constituencies. As a result the aforementioned examples are select and not encompassing of the issues and topics to which women federal legislators have lent their support.

CONCLUSION

Women, minorities, and minority women remain underrepresented in legislative bodies. Within the federal legislative body especially, women, minorities, and minority women remain in numbers below that of their actual numbers within the American electorate and overall citizenry. Although women have not gained critical mass within legislative bodies, they have proven that they are committed to supporting those causes that impact the well-being of women and families such as equal pay, childcare, and gun control. As issues such as reproductive rights command the attention of media, women voters, and their families, women in the federal legislative, in particular, will undoubtedly become central players in the associated debates or discourse. They have also demonstrated that they are willing to engage in those issues that have been historically deemed "non-women's" issues such as consumer finance. Hence, women within the federal legislative-making body have demonstrated that they are just as, if not more, willing to actively engage in those debates that shape the laws and policies that govern the entire American electorate.

Legislators of color have also demonstrated substantive representation of racial and ethnic minorities, as issues specific to communities of color continue to persist due to the vestiges of racism that continue to pervade structures and systems despite the occasional assertion of a post-racial nation. Aside from the obvious concerns racism presents, the evolution of the United States into a racially and ethnically diverse country will mean that matters salient to racial and ethnic minorities become priorities, or even mandates, requiring legislative attention. Due to advances in technology and social media, the attention of the general citizenry is focusing increasingly more on race relations and the role of race in societal sectors and institutions such as education, health, and the labor force. Correspondingly, it would only be logical that the increasingly diversifying electorate demand accountability from those they have elected to represent their interests.

However, women legislators of color have both supported and introduced legislation and/or resolutions that seek to aid women, men, and families of diverse backgrounds. In viewing the statements of women of color within the federal legislative body, it is apparent that they possess a distinctively comprehensive view of issues that impact individuals and communities on a daily basis. Even more so, in their support of various legislation and resolutions, they acknowledge the roles of race and/or gender as they influence the lived experiences of individuals within larger social and economic institutions. For this reason, their lived experiences as members of two marginalized groups makes them uniquely qualified to represent a broad scale of constituents.

Again, as observed by Pearson and Dancey, that women and women of color are more apt to give floor speeches and engage in debates increases their visibility among the electorate (2011). Potentially, this aids in the minimizing or erasing of stereotypes that prevent women from being viewed as leaders. Over time, it is quite plausible that seeing women as governmental leaders will facilitate greater acceptance of a woman occupying the U.S. Presidency. Going a step further, it is quite plausible that, in time, women of color serving in legislative bodies will increasingly be perceived as competent leaders willing to represent the interests of persons with various backgrounds.

NOTE

1. Congresswoman Barbara Lee's quote cites 78 cents for every dollar which is one cent higher than the evidence presented earlier in the chapter.

Chapter 3

Through the Lens of Black Women
The Significance of Obama's Campaign

In 2008, for the first time in the history of the United States, an African-American man was elected to the Presidency of the United States. Faced with this awe-inspiring moment in history, it goes without saying that many African-Americans were, and continue to be, filled with a renewed sense of pride. Many were also inspired by the campaign of former U.S. Senator and Secretary of State Hillary Clinton. Because of the unprecedented nature of both campaigns, members of the media and "everyday" citizens began to have open dialogues about the issues of race and gender within the national political arena. For some, the success of President Obama's campaign brought to mind the idea of an African-American woman one day securing the nomination of a major political party.

As discussed in Chapter 1, black women have been intricately involved in American politics for decades—both indirectly and directly. Despite often filling the role of political and social advocate, organizer, or activist, black women remain disproportionately underrepresented in elected offices on the state and national levels. Even during Reconstruction, a time marked by a historic surge in the election of blacks to state and national offices, no black women were elected in large part, due to the fact that women were not extended the right to vote until 1920. Thus, women did not have a visible role in the political arena at that time; causing many women to engage in the suffragist movement that was often hostile toward women of color. Compounding matters, the surge in the number of black elected officials came to a screeching halt with the end of Reconstruction (Harrison 2008; Burton 1978).

Because black women have long faced the dual challenges of racism and sexism, it was not until the second half of the twentieth century that Shirley Chisolm was elected to the United States House of Representatives (Congressional Office of History and Preservation 2014). Since that time, very few black women have effectively participated in national politics (Congressional Office of History and Preservation 2014). From the time of its inception, over 12,000 men and women have served in the United States Congress collectively. However, only 30 of those have been black women—a percentage that can be described as miniscule at best (Office of History and Preservation 2016).

RACE TO THE 44TH U.S. PRESIDENCY

As the media and others intricately examined the impact of race and gender on the voting trends of Americans in general, many became increasingly fascinated by the voting trends of African-Americans during the Democratic primaries. While some wondered if African Americans would take a chance on the candidate widely perceived as a political newcomer, others wondered if African-Americans would support former Senator Clinton out of allegiance to former President Bill Clinton. During his terms as president, Bill Clinton was widely embraced by members of the African-American community (Freeman 2008). Nonetheless, after each primary, the same trends emerged time and again. Consistently, the vast majority of African-Americans voted for now President Barack Obama while many white women voted for Senator Hillary Clinton. Data released by the Gallup Poll illustrated that African-American men and women were significantly more likely to support President Obama than former U.S. Senator and Secretary of State Clinton (Newport and Saad 2008). Additionally, the data demonstrated that white women were more likely to support Senator Clinton at a two to one margin (Newport and Saad 2008).

At one point during the Democratic primaries, some questioned the role of African-American women's voting patterns. Many wondered if African-American women would vote according to their race or according to their gender. This question shed light on the unique position of African-American women. For some, this question has shed light on the role of African-American women as candidates or contenders in the political arena.

BLACK WOMEN'S PERCEPTIONS AND OBSERVATIONS

Although African-American women have played an integral role in the political arena for many years, none have been considered as a potential nominee of a major, national political party. As such, the respective candidacies of an African-American man and a white woman provoked the question, "How long before we see an African-American woman as the nominee of a major, national political party?" Thus, one must ask: (1) What sociohistorical forces facilitated this moment in history?; (2) Will these same forces pave the way for a woman of color? Why? Why not?; (3) How long will it take from the 2008 Democratic Primaries to witness such an occasion?; and (4) Will it happen in our lifetime? In response to these questions, two focus groups comprised solely of black women ranging in ages 21–44 were conducted during the latter part of the 2007–2008 Democratic primary season to explore the significance of Obama's campaign through their lenses (Table 3.1).[1]

Moderator's Guide

The moderator's guide began by querying participants' general views on the 2007–2008 Democratic primaries. The guide continued to explore the roles of race and gender in the primaries followed by an exploration of the unique role of African-American women in the political arena. Moreover, although the moderator's guide queried participants on their perceptions of Obama's campaign in the context of race and gender, the guide also queried participants on their overall view of the presidential election on future generations of voters.

It is important to acknowledge that data collected from focus groups and other forms of qualitative research cannot be generalized to a specified population. A focus group is not a statistically significant representation of

Table 3.1 Focus Group Participants by Occupation and Age

Participant	Focus Group 1	Participant	Focus Group 2
1	Occupation: Vault Teller Age: 27	1	Occupation: Doctoral Student Age: 27
2	Occupation: Administrative Assistant Age: 35	2	Occupation: Doctoral Student Age: 26
3	Occupation: Early Learning Teacher Age: 23	3	Occupation: Education Research Consultant Age: 44
4	Occupation: Unemployed Age: 35	4	Occupation: Health and Wellness Coordinator Age: 31
5	Occupation: Special Education Aide Age: 23	5	Occupation: IT Consultant Age: 38
6	Occupation: Center Director, Early Head Start Program Age: 27	6	Occupation: Cable News Producer Age: 30
7	Occupation: Staff Assistant Age: 21		

a population. However, it consists of a group of persons selected from the population being studied, and it can be used to learn topics of concern to that population.

General Perceptions of the 2007–2008 Democratic Primary Season

Overall, the majority of focus group participants indicated that they closely followed the events of the 2007–2008 Democratic primary season. Not surprisingly, the majority of participants in both focus groups described the primary season as "exciting." Focus group participants were equally enthusiastic about the Democratic Party candidates. For the most part, participants in both focus groups expressed enthusiasm for the historical importance of the 2007–2008 Democratic primaries. For instance, when asked if they thought they would ever see a woman or a black man contending for the nomination of a national political party, participants in both focus groups exclaimed in virtual unison, "Never!" One participant further stated, "Both candidates [were] shocking."

Accordingly, a couple of the respondents in the first focus group commented on the racial and gender undertones historically associated with the presidency. One commented, "[It is] all about white men. We're so close minded." Another commented, "Society has us believing that only white men should have it." One participant continued to say that she was equally shocked that Obama had not been sabotaged. As she explained,

> I always thought they would undermine him before anyone knew a black man was running. You know, find some way to say that he was not eligible . . .

Similarly, a couple of the respondents in the second focus group commented, "I never thought it would happen in my lifetime." One participant further commented, "we've jumped from being three-fifths of a person to a . . . black president" followed by another respondent commenting, "We've really only been voting for 50 years." Another respondent explained,

> [I] didn't even think of [Obama's candidacy] as an option. [I was] more surprised to see Obama than Clinton. Looking at the Clinton legacy, this is what [Hillary Clinton] has been striving for since her husband was president. It seems as if Obama just came out of no where.

Participants attributed the success of Obama's campaign to a few sociohistorical forces. Although a couple of participants in the first focus group attributed the success of Obama's campaign to an overall lack of satisfaction with the Bush administration, other participants in the first focus group attributed the success to an increase in racial tolerance. For example, one participant stated, "Society is less focused on race. [Obama] has a lot of white supporters." Ironically, in response to the sentiments of greater racial tolerance, another participant in the first focus group attributed Obama's success to his gender indicating that gender bias may have played an integral role. The participant remarked, ". . . I think it also has to do with him being a man. A lot of older men think women are too emotional . . . ."

Similar to participants in the first focus group, participants in the second focus group also identified the failures of the Bush administration as a sociohistorical force that have facilitated the success of the Obama campaign. More specifically, participants in the second group indicated that the Bush administration's untimely and inadequate response to the victims of Hurricane Katrina stirred visceral emotions among many persons of color. Focus group participants in the second focus group explained that,

> Many people felt disenfranchised after Katrina. Therefore, people are looking for someone else to lead who doesn't look like those who failed to lead after Hurricane Katrina.

Participants' comments pertained to the events following Hurricane Katrina, that many perceived convincingly shed light on the significant divisions related to race and class within the United States. For weeks following the hurricane, media images illustrated predominantly low-income, African-Americans literally awaiting rescue on the rooftops of their water logged homes in an effort to survive. Even more upsetting to the scores of persons watching the events unfold on television and the internet was the federal government's response to those trying to survive. To countless persons, the government's response time was unacceptable, and to some degree, motivated by the demographics of those in need (Henkel, Dovidio, and Gaertner 2006).

Caught Between Race and Gender?

Participants in both focus groups were asked their thoughts on the media's initial claims that African-American women were in a uniquely difficult position due to their race and gender. Thus, participants were explicitly asked if they ever felt conflicted between their race and their gender at any point in the course of the primaries. While none of the participants in the second focus group responded that they never experienced any internal conflict, a couple of participants in the second focus group said that they initially felt conflicted between their race and their gender. As one participant observed,

> After I thought about it, for a black man, that means we've come a looooong way. Although women are still a minority, I think black people are at a greater disadvantage than white women.

For this reason, this particular participant indicated that she decided to support Obama. Further exploring the role of gender, respondents were asked what role they believed gender played during the most recent Democratic primary season. While one or two participants in each focus group said that gender played an integral role, the majority of respondents in both focus groups indicated that race played a more integral role than gender. As one participant commented, "I think Obama's blackness helped him. It helped to distinguish him." Other participants commented, "[I believe] the older blacks voted for him because they thought they would never see this happen."

Consequently, respondents in the first focus group commented on Obama's precarious position as president. Specifically, focus group participants explained that, because Obama is an African-American, he will be held to a higher standard than past presidents who were all white. As one participant explained, "He's going to be criticized more because of who he is—a black man." Participants continued to explain that Obama will have to produce or do everything that he has promised while campaigning. Comments made by focus group participants to this effect included, "They're going to watch his every move" as well as "Everything he has said he is going to have to execute because of who he is."

Perceptions of African-American Women and the U.S. Presidency

When asked how Obama's and/or Clinton's respective campaigns have paved the way for African-American women who wish to seek the nomination of a national political party, there were distinct differences overall between the two focus groups. Participants in the first focus group expressed that both Obama and Clinton have made great inroads for such a possibility. As pointed out by one participant in the first focus group, "[Both of them] definitely opened doors—whether for a woman or an African-American."

As the discussion began to focus primarily on African-American women, there were mixed reactions among participants in the first focus group as to whether or not an African-American woman would have an easier chance of attaining the nomination of a major political party as a result of the 2007–2008 Democratic primaries. While one participant contended that an African-American woman would "have a great chance," other participants contended the opposite. For instance, one participant asserted, "the stigma will always be there. In some people's eyes, it's not meant for us to succeed." Another participant in the same way observed,

> She would be a black woman—a double negative. Being a woman, you have to prove yourself against a man. Being black, you have to prove yourself against whites. She would have to work harder than Obama and Clinton. But (Obama and Clinton) will make it more likely.

Correspondingly, participants in the second focus group contended, "There is no paving the way." As another participant agreed stating, "Look at what they are doing to [Michelle Obama], and she has the skill set of anybody running." One more participant concluded, "There is no pleasing (society). We will always be painted as angry black women."

Participants were referring to the media's response to Mrs. Obama's statements to the media regarding what she described as an overwhelming, unprecedented since of pride in her country. In response to her statements, many in the mainstream media labeled her as unpatriotic and angry (Post 2009). There were additional instances in which the media's racially tinged perceptions of Mrs. Obama surfaced. Most prominent was the media's reference to Mrs. Obama as then Senator Obama's "baby mama," failing to acknowledge their, at the time, 16-year legal marriage (Post 2009).

Participants in the first focus group continued to assert that no social factor in particular would have to be in place to facilitate an African-American woman's attainment of a major political party nomination. In fact, one participant contended that the Republican Party would support Condoleezza Rice, Secretary of State, if she sought the presidency. However, participants also noted that Condoleezza Rice would win the nomination only if there were no other pool of viable candidates from which to choose. Participants' sentiment regarding Secretary Rice's nomination barring no other viable candidates may stem from what has been described as an overall lack of minority representation within the Republican Party (Heppen 2003). Indeed, the Republican Party has been under increasing criticism in recent years for its lack of racial and ethnic diversity (Benedetto 2005). Issues comprising the Republican Party's platform also tend to contradict those issues important to African-Americans (Wallace et al. 2009).

Participants in both focus groups were asked to identify what barriers or stereotypes in particular they believe would hinder an African-American woman's aspirations of attaining the nomination of a major political party. Although a couple of participants said that they believe stereotypes associated with African-American women cannot be overcome, one participant stated,

Positive [black female] role models still portray the stereotypes of black women. Look at Oprah . . . We still need [to exhibit] those stereotypes. The neck rolling . . . The outspokenness . . . That's how we show our strength.

Even so, while participants in the first focus group asserted that certain stereotypes associated with African-American are manifestations of the emotional and mental strength of African-American women, participants in the second focus group asserted that these same stereotypes are indeed prohibitive to the professional aspirations of African-American women.

In fact, participants identified stereotypes that exist in and outside of the African-American community. In terms of the stereotypes that exist within the African-American community, one participant stated, "[In order to win the nomination of a major political party], we would have to overcome the misogyny." Another participant contended, "Black men only see us as sex objects or caregivers there to serve them." In terms of stereotypes that exist outside of the African-American community, one participant stated, "White people look at us as mammy, b*tchy, or loose and dirty." Along the same vein, another participant stated, "White men look at us as a 'romp in the jungle.'" Such views may provide some context to results of a study conducted by Philpot and Walton (2007). In examining the likelihood of voters' support of a black female candidate by race and gender, Philpot and Walton determined that black female candidates were likely to gain extraordinary levels of support from other black women. Black men were also likely to support black female candidates if the other candidate was not a black male. Thus, within the black community, black female candidates continue to face issues associated with their gender. Study investigators also discerned that black female candidates were not likely to attract white male and female voters at the same level of black female voters. Only when the black female candidate had an extensive amount of political experience did white male and female voters support black female candidates.

The Next Generation

Participants were asked to describe the impact of Obama's successful campaign on the political participation of minority populations. Overall, the vast majority of participants said that there would be a positive effect on the political participation of minorities as a result of Obama's successful campaign. Still, participants observed that the 2008 Democratic primary season sparked unprecedented passions and excitement among many Americans. As one participant commented, "I think black people are more passionate than ever because we've never gotten this far before."

Moreover, while one participant said that Obama's and Clinton's efforts have made her believe "I can do anything I want to," another participant said that Obama's and Clinton's efforts have made her "more aware and more confident." Likewise, a participant in the second focus group said that Obama's and Clinton's efforts have helped. As the participant explained, "Any time you see yourself in a candidate, it will definitely catch the attention of those who feel disenfranchised."

Overall, upon reading the reactions of focus group participants, it can be deduced that they were quite excited about the 2007–2008 Democratic primaries. The excitement exhibited by participants may be attributed to the success and potential promise of the first Obama presidential campaign. While participants acknowledged the historical importance of Clinton's candidacy, participants in general contended that the gains and successes of the first Obama campaign are of even greater, historical importance. Specifically, participants contended that, in comparison to their white counterparts, African-Americans remain at a disadvantage. Therefore, although they were proud to see a woman make great strides in the national political arena, they were more proud to see an African-American man make significant strides in the national political arena.

Still, one must contemplate what the 2008 primaries and the 2012 U.S. presidential elections mean for women and women of color. Participants in both focus groups explained that, in comparison to Obama and Clinton, an African-American woman seeking the presidential nomination of a major political party would face the cumulative effects of race and gender. Even so, because of the achievements of Obama and Clinton, some focus group participants indicated that an African-American woman may one day have a greater chance of securing the nomination of a major political party.

NOTE

1. A convenience sampling approach was utilized to recruit focus group participants. All of those recruited to participate in the focus group were African-American, female, self-identified member of the Democratic Party, and at least 18 years of age. Education and/or income level were not criteria for selection.

Chapter 4

Race and Gender in National Politics

The Origins and Intersection of the Two

Focus group analyses in Chapter 3 revealed that the socially constructed stigmas associated with race and gender continue to pervade the political arena. Still, focus group participants expressed a palpable sense of hope regarding a greater inclusiveness of those who have been historically marginalized. Nonetheless, focus group participants remained adamant that, despite the historical significance of the 2008 primaries and the collective political progress made by people of color with the election of President Obama, the intersecting realities of gender and race would continue to overshadow the political legacies of black women especially.

HISTORICAL AND ONGOING ROLE OF GENDER

From the inception of the United States government, gender has been an unavoidable topic. In fact, the persons who are often credited for developing the framework of the United States' government are often affectionately referred to as the "Founding Fathers"—one could argue a verbal yet blatantly symbolic nod to the patriarchal supremacy existing within and throughout American government. Aside from the symbolic terminology often utilized to reference the framers of the United States government, the actual authors of the United States Constitution, at times, employed terminology that reflected an unambiguous view of gender and government leadership. Explicitly, as an example, in establishing the office of the United States Presidency, the authors of the United States Constitution clearly articulated,

The executive Power shall be vested in a President of the United States of America. *He* shall hold *his* Office during the Term of four Years, and, together with the Vice President, chosen for the same Term, be elected. (emphasis added)

The authors of the Constitution made evident that the democratic process was exclusive to select members of the citizenry. Such codified language seemingly set the tone for many years to come, as the systemic exclusion of women from the formal democratic process has persisted. It was not until the ratification of the 19th Amendment 133 years after the inception of the U.S. Constitution that women were granted the right to vote.

According to statistics released by the most recent U.S. Census, females comprise 50.8 percent of the United States population (2015). Logically, because political officeholders are elected to serve as representatives of a larger citizenry, one would assume that such persons would reflect those they are to represent. But, in comparison to men, women remain disproportionably underrepresented in politics, especially on the state and national levels. One of the most revealing examples of female under representation on the state level is the gender composition of United States' governors. Taking a glance at all of the currently serving state governors, one can quickly ascertain the scant number of women with only five of the 50 being women (Center for American Women in Politics 2015).

The same pattern emerges when looking at female representation within state legislatures. At present, men continue to occupy the majority of seats within state legislatures with men occupying over 80 percent in some states (Center for American Women in Politics 2015). In a 2001 study, the origins of female under representation on the state level were explored utilizing data from the General Social Survey (GSS), 1974–1996. Upon an analysis of data collected from 38 states, the study investigator determined that attitudes toward gender roles remain germane to candidate selection in the twenty-first century. Moreover, the study's author noted that states with multimember districts were more likely to have greater female representation versus those states that did not have multimember districts (Arceneux 2001). Multimember districts are those districts that are represented by more than one person within the state legislature, although the election to select representatives is a competitive one. Because multimember districts allow for the selection of multiple representatives, the author posited that it is possible that voters are likely to select a female candidate when a male candidate could be selected as well (Arceneux 2001).

A look at women politicians serving on the national level reveals a similar trend. Of the 435 persons comprising the United States House of Representatives, less than a quarter are women. Although a greater proportion than that currently serving in the lower chamber of the House, the 40 percent of women currently serving in the Senate still fails to reflect the little over 50 percent of women that comprise the overall United States population. A closer look at the individual states reveals that, to date, one state-Iowa—has never elected a woman to the U.S. House of Representatives or Senate. Moreover, there are currently 12 states that have no female representation within either chamber of the U.S. Congress.

A plethora of earlier studies explored the role of gender in politics (Lawless 2004; Oxley and Fox 2004; Milyo and and Schosberg 2000; Cole and Stewart 1996; Witt, Paget, and Matthews 1995; Moncrief and Thompson 1991). Earlier studies consistently revealed that a candidate's gender proved to be a germane point of consideration when voters select a candidate. Political and social scientists continue to conduct countless studies in order to determine the incontrovertible role of gender in choosing a political candidate (Dolan 2014; Fox and Lawless 2014; Fulton, 2012; Sklar 2008; Dolan 2005).

Prior to becoming a candidate, one must make the assumingly arduous decision to run for office. Analyses have therefore also attempted to identify, and potentially explain, the genesis of the gender gap within the political arena (Fox and Lawless 2014; Ford 2011). A recent study, for instance, specifically sought to examine a potential disparity in political ambition among male and female high school and college students. Study investigators discovered that male students had contemplated a career in politics at a greater rate than female students (Fox and Lawless 2014). As logically expected, the disparity in political ambition was not attributable to biology alone. Study investigators determined that political socialization was integral to one's consideration of a career in politics (i.e., encouragement from parents and friends, engaging in politically oriented conversations with family and friends, etc.). As a result, study investigators concluded that females also exhibited a high probability of contemplating political careers if they too were politically socialized. For some reason however, males were more likely to experience political social-ization than females, and the socialization was more likely to occur during college years (Fox and Lawless 2014). Such findings point to an ongoing practice of society, whether intentional or unintentional, to groom men more so than women for political careers. Thus, political and social scientists remain vigilant in identifying the genesis of gender bias in elections.

In identifying the origins of such gender bias, political and social scientists have sought to delve into the function of gender stereotypes in voter percep-tions and subsequent candidate selection. Expressly, gender stereotypes in the context of standard candidate traits such as perceived intelligence, experience in political office, trustworthiness, critical thinking skills, ideologies, and so on. have revealed ongoing disparities in voter perceptions (Fulton 2012; Ford 2011; Sanbonmatsu and Dolan 2009; Dolan 2005). Women are viewed as more compassionate and men are perceived as more managerial. As measured via various studies, even voters' perceptions of policy issues remain gendered (Dolan 2010; Dolan 2005). On a broad scale, voters tend to view some policy issues as being innately female while others are innately male (Lawless 2004). Such topics, including the economy and terrorism, are often perceived by voters to be better addressed by men than women (Dolan 2010). Female candidates for this reason are more likely to be subjected to a disparate level of scrutiny in comparison to their male counterparts in regard to issues that impact the safety and financial well-being of the public on the national level. Consequently, while women have made some strides in terms of political representation, the existing post-9/11 environment may make overcoming gender under representation especially challenging (Dolan 2010, Lawless 2004). Indeed, candidates' respective capabilities in terms of international relations, and terrorism chiefly, were often the focus of voters and media pundits during the course of the 2008 Democratic presidential primary season. Candidates were frequently asked how they would curb and/or prevent possible terrorist violence to U.S. citizens because of the ongoing angst of many since the attacks of September 11, 2001. Although the events of September 11th created what has been labeled a "new norm" in terms of living under the constant threat of terrorist attacks on U.S. soil, it was during the 2008 Presidential Primaries that then presidential candidate Hillary Clinton was criticized for her vote to go to war with Iraq while serving in the U.S. Senate (Rucker 2014). As a consequence, while men are often expected to take stereotypically aggressive stances, Clinton, often times, was criticized for being to aggressive, and accordingly, in violation of gendered social norms.

HISTORICAL AND ONGOING ROLE OF RACE

As noted in the previous chapter, the election of President Barack Obama was a dream realized for many blacks within the United States. Just as gender has proven to be a challenging factor in the national political arena, so has race. Like the language used by the authors of the Constitution to exclude women from the democratic process, the language used by the authors to refer to persons of color were in no way inclusive. In fact, at the time Constitution was written, many of the authors themselves, were ironically slave owners (O'Reilly 1999). In referencing enslaved blacks within the Constitution, the authors utilized a fraction—three-fifths. Plainly stated, black persons were considered less than a person, and were in fact, considered property for the purposes of taxation. As stated in Article I,

> Representatives and direct Taxes shall be apportioned among the several States which may be included within this Union, according to their respective

Numbers, which shall be determined by adding to the whole Number of free persons, including those bound to Service for a Term of Years, and excluding Indians not taxed, three fifths of all other Persons.

Therefore, just as the authors of the Constitution employed less than gender neutral language that shaped and influenced the male to female ratio within political institutions, the language used to describe black persons established a foundation for many years of political inequality to follow. It was not until the ratification of the 14th and 15th Amendments that black persons were recognized as citizens and granted the right to vote, respectively. Nevertheless, as noted above, women were not granted the right to vote until the 19th Amendment. Therefore, even with the incorporation of the 15th Amendment, only black men were granted the right to vote.

With the ratification of the 13th, 14th, and 15th Amendments, also known as the Civil Rights Amendments, a new era in democracy began. The era, termed Reconstruction, witnessed the introduction of black men elected to state legislatures. Unfortunately, the era of Reconstruction was short-lived due to the Compromise of 1877 that ended the occupation of federal soldiers in southern states (Forner 2000). Once Reconstruction came to an end, so did too the increasing representation of blacks in elected offices (Forner 2002). What is more, for almost the next 100 years, blacks were effectively disenfranchised from the democratic process (Terrell 2005; Forner 2002; Prestage 1991; Branch 1988).

It was the systemic disenfranchisement of blacks from the democratic process that ushered in the Civil Rights Movement of the 1950s and 1960s, a time period popularly marked by collective and personal sacrifice, public protests, and unified struggle (Giddens 2006). Eventually, the Civil Rights Movement birthed the landmark Voting Rights Act of 1965 that granted the right to vote regardless of race, religion, national origin, age, or sex. Like the Reconstruction Era, the post-modern Civil Rights Movement witnessed a demonstrable increase in the number of blacks elected to public offices (Chisolm 2010; Anderson-Bricker 1999). Yet, the number of blacks elected to public state and national office since the ratification of the 1964 Civil Rights Act and the 1965 Voting Rights Act remains disproportionately low in comparison to the percentage and/or number of blacks comprising the United States citizenry. Despite the Civil Rights and Voting Rights Acts, persons of color and, blacks especially, continue to be subjected to both prejudice and discrimination in various forms. The legacies of de jure practices such as slavery and Jim Crow have left an undeniable scourge on the manner in which black persons are received within society as a whole. Social psychology and communication scholars have repeatedly measured the effects of skin color on the perceptions of individuals in order to detect the possible existence of stereotyping.

Such efforts have overwhelmingly revealed biases against those of African descent, as study results consistently show that persons with dark skin color often have the labels lazy, criminal, unintelligent, and untrustworthy attached to them (Feldman 2010; Eberhardt 2010; Iyengar 2010).

2008 Racial and Political Perspectives

Taking the above into consideration and using data collected as part of the 2008 Collaborative Multi-Racial Post-Election Survey (CMPS), the perceptions of men and women of varying races and ethnicities were analyzed. The CMPS, a national telephone survey of registered voters, was conducted by the Inter-university Consortium for Political and Social Research from November 2008 to January 2009 following the historic 2008 election. The survey gleaned reactions to, and perceptions of, the 2008 election from representative samples of Asians, blacks, Hispanics/Latinos, and whites ages 18 and up (University of Michigan 2008). The survey probed multiple topics related to the 2008 primary season and general election. For example, respondents were probed on multiple social issues that arose during the 2008 primary season and general election. Notably, respondents were asked about their perceptions of racial relations and minority groups within the United States.

As such, one of the questions posed to survey respondents focused on one stereotype often attributed to blacks (see Table 4.1). Specifically, survey respondents ($n = 4,335$) were asked if they believe "blacks work hard." In response, close to 30 percent ($n = 1,286$) indicated that "almost all" or "most blacks work hard" while the remaining majority stated that "some," "few," or "almost no blacks work hard." Respondents were also asked if they believe blacks are "easy to get along with." Slightly more than half of respondents (56 percent) indicated that "almost all blacks" ($n = 1,077$) or "most blacks" ($n = 1,501$) are "easy to get along with." The remaining 44 percent of survey participants responded "some blacks," "few blacks,"

Table 4.1   Respondent Perceptions: Blacks Work Hard by Gender

	Gender		
	Women	Men	Total
Almost All Blacks	364	246	610
Most Blacks	723	563	1286
Some Blacks	838	667	1505
Few Blacks	240	183	423
Almost No Blacks	56	42	98
Don't Know/Missing	373	268	641
Total	2,594	1,969	4,563

"almost no blacks," or simply "don't know" in regard to blacks being "easy to get along with."

Black Politicians

Accordingly, black persons must contend with the daily realities of resisting and overcoming such generalizations. Notably, black politicians seeking elected office must identify methods of overcoming the historical marginalization of racial and ethnic minorities in the United States (Vesla 2012). In this manner, since the passage of the Voting Rights Act of 1965, social and political scholars have looked at the experiences of blacks within the political arena. Among the types of studies that have been conducted, white voters' perceptions of and willingness to vote for black candidates, specifically, have been the more popular subtopics in terms of blacks' pursuit of elected office. Thus, in seeking to pinpoint the genesis of white voters' hesitance to vote for black candidates, on the state and national levels primarily, numerous studies have queried potential voters and conducted retrospective analyses of elections involving black candidates in an effort to identify ways in which to increase the number of successful black candidates. Jeffries and Jones, for example, conducted a series of interviews in an addition to a content analysis of statewide elections held between 1966 and 2006, in order to identify ways to increase the acceptability of black candidates on a broader scale. Of the studies' conclusions, the need to appear "race neutral" was paramount, or primarily, not restricted to those issues largely viewed as "black issues" (2006). Ironically, although the Civil Rights Era was central to asserting the political power of blacks in an attempt to create an authentically democratic government, other political scholars have supported the notion that black candidates must refrain from associating themselves with the politics and events of the Civil Rights Era in order to appeal to a mainstream audience. Failing to do so in the course of state or national elections, may alienate voters, white voters explicitly, who may view such as candidates as radical or militant. This was the case of L. Douglas Wilder, the first black governor of Virginia, who, unlike presidential candidates the Reverends Jesse Jackson and Al Sharpton, took great strides during his campaign to disassociate himself from the Civil Rights Era and to portray himself as a candidate whose stance on social issues largely coincided with the general or mainstream electorate of Virginia (Jeffries 1999).

Such was also the case of now President Barack Obama. Early in his campaign, he took great effort to portray himself as a candidate who, like many others regardless of skin color, was a product of the American dream. He just happened to be black—the product of an interracial marriage between a white woman and a Kenyan man. Throughout his campaign, President Obama repeatedly spoke about being raised by his single mother and grandparents. He also emphasized his hard work in and commitment to earning his undergraduate and law degrees at top schools (Wise 2009). In discussing his postsecondary and postgraduate matriculation, he commonly referred to his and his wife's need to take out student loans—words and actions identifiable with many middle-class Americans. President Obama's description of his upbringing was, for the most part, effective in portraying him as a presidential candidate who reflected the American traditions of individual agency and hard work, and who again, just happened to be black. In spite of his efforts to paint himself as a "colorless" or "race neutral" candidate, many insisted on focusing on his apparent racial background. In fact, U.S. Senator Harry Reid made headlines when it was discovered that he, when giving what he believed to be a statement of support to then Senator Obama, said that, "he believed that the country was ready to embrace a black presidential candidate, especially one such as Obama—a light-skinned African-American with no Negro dialect, unless he wanted one" (Ciliizza 2010). Senator Reid's comments, while shocking, reflect the prevailing cultural perceptions regarding race within the United States' political arena. More so, Senator Reid's comments about now President Obama's skin tone affirm widespread perceptions of skin color as a proxy for personality traits, and thus, further support existing empirical evidence reflecting society's continued rejection of darker skin tones. Senator Reid was not alone in his comments regarding President Obama's racial identity. Numerous people often commented on Obama's "exotic" background in an attempt to make him appear different or unique regardless of his narrative of being raised by a single mother, paying his own way through school, and remaining married to the professionally accomplished mother of his two children. In short, as much as Obama reiterated his likeness to many Americans, he was still effectively made to be the "other." There also were, and continue to be, more overt racist comments made about President Obama. In addition to the usual racial epithets used to deride black Americans, verbal and written comments have compared him to a monkey or other primitive animal, accused him of being a terrorist, and called for violent physical attacks to be made against the Commander in Chief (Brown 2014).

HISTORICAL AND ONGOING CUMULATIVE EFFECTS OF RACE *AND* GENDER

As noted previously, the U.S. Constitution granted blacks the right to vote with the ratification of the 15th Amendment. Even still, because the 19th amendment was not ratified until significantly later, black women were not permitted to vote until the early part of the twentieth century (Giddings

2006). As referenced in Chapter 1, while working to obtain suffrage rights for women, black women were habitually made to feel not welcomed by white women though sharing the same gender, and therefore, working for the same goal (Giddens 2006). In the face of such paradoxical discrimination, black women continued to work for the enfranchisement and suffrage of all persons, and blacks principally, via both informal and formal networks and mechanisms. Ultimately, as widely known, the organized efforts of black women and other persons brought about the manifestation of the Civil Rights Act of 1964 and the Voting Rights Act of 1965. The experience they accumulated working in the various humanitarian and civil rights organizations as organizers and educators made them prime candidates to represent those communities with whom they had worked to engage in the democratic process. Not to mention, the passage of the Voting Rights Act served as a catalyst for the creation of majority black districts. It was from these districts that most black women, on the heels of the Voting Rights Act of 1965, were elected to state and national legislative bodies (Chisolm 2010; Darcy and Hadley 1987).

However, as noted in the previous chapter, they continue to be represented within the national legislative houses in miniscule numbers (Center for American Woman and Politics 2015; Center for American Women and Politics 2014). Since the naissance of the U.S. House of Representatives, less than one percent of the total persons who have served there have been both black and female, and only one black woman has served in the U.S. Senate in its history. Needless to say, although white women must contend with sexism and men of color must contend with racism, women of color in the political arena are faced with what has been termed a "double disadvantage." The dual identity of black women was explored by Moncrief and Thompson as an application of the "double disadvantage hypothesis," As part of their analysis of state legislators' respective backgrounds, Moncrief and Thompson discovered that, in general, the educational backgrounds and credentials of black women exceeded those of their black male, white male, and white female counterparts. Study results also revealed that black women were more likely to have more prestigious occupations than their black male, white male, and white female counterparts (1991). As such, study results suggest that, in order to be considered suitable for election to political offices, black women must be better prepared academically and professionally in order to overcome the reciprocal effects of racism and sexism. Nonetheless, because black women were elected to the U.S. Congress due to the creation of majority black districts as byproducts of the Voting Rights Act of 1965 remains a daunting reality. To be more pointed, to many, black women lack the broad or wide-scale appeal necessary to secure an increased number of seats in the U.S. Congress or to secure the presidential nomination of a major political party. Once again, reflecting the results of Moncrief and Thompson's study, Philpot and Walton concluded that white men and women were more likely to support a black female candidate if she had extensive experience (see Chapter 3).

The hesitance of black voters in Philpot and Walton's 2007 study are reflective of earlier findings revealed as part of the 1993 National Black Politics Study. Of the 1,206 black persons surveyed, three-quarters agreed that "black women should share equally in the political leadership of the black community." A sizable proportion of 19 percent, however, agreed with the statement, "black women should not undermine black male leadership." These findings are somewhat astonishing considering approximately half of those surveyed also agreed with the statement, "black women have suffered from both sexism within the black movement and racism within the women's movement." All the same, such contradictory and patriarchal perspectives, in part, contribute to the marginalization of black women within the political arena and provide greater context to the unique position of black women within the political arena despite their long-standing tradition of public service and leadership. As an example, in 2016, former District of Columbia Mayor Vincent Gray opted to challenge his once protégé and loyal supporter, Ward 7 Councilwoman Yvette Alexander, for her seat on the District of Columbia Council in lieu of challenging the at-large incumbent Vincent Orange, a black man (Schwartzman and Hauslohner 2016). It has been speculated that the former mayor's pursuit of Councilwoman Alexander's seat is part of his overall strategy to reclaim the position of mayor currently held by Muriel Bowser, a black woman that Gray has openly criticized (Hauslohner 2016; Schwartzman 2015). Gray's choice to pursue Alexander's seat is undoubtedly due to polls that showed he had a greater chance of winning against Alexander than Orange (Hauslohner 2016). The polls proved to be correct. On Tuesday, June 14, 2016, Vincent Gray beat out Yvette Alexander in the Democratic Primary in a landslide victory. Because Washington, DC, is a largely Democratic area, he will most assuredly win the seat on the council in November 2016.

Upon conducting a multivariate analysis of religious involvement on the political engagement of African-American men and women, Robnett and Bany, like Fox and Lawless, posited that African-American males may receive more encouragement than African-American women to become directly involved in political activities (2011). The authors noted that, since the passage of the Voting Rights Act of 1965, African-American women are not as visible in the political sphere as they were during the 1960s and 1970s. Granted, Robnett and Bany contended that African-American women are more likely to vote than African-American males, but the authors speculated that the patriarchal nature of social institutions within communities of color, such as the church, may be one mediating factor involving the gender gap in political leadership among African-Americans.

However, just as black women candidates must contend with the patriarchy existent within black communities, they must also contend with common racial stereotypes within their gender (see Table 4.2). Hence, again using data collected as part of the 2008 CMPS, the racial perceptions of white, Hispanic, and Asian women were explored. In order to compare and contrast the perceptions of Asian, Hispanic, and white women, the responses of those who self—identified as "female" were selected for subsequent, inferential analyses. Upon selecting those who self-identified as "female," there were over 2,500 respondents ($n = 2,594$) comprising the subsample including 447 Asians, 605 blacks, 915 Hispanics/Latinas, and 627 whites.

Although jobs and the economy were deemed to be a far greater decisive factor in determining how to cast their respective votes, race relations ranked among issues of relevance among the total subsample of women. When asked about specific minority groups, and blacks in particular, there was definitely differences by racial group. The majority of Asian women expressed less than positive views when asked if they believe "blacks work hard" (see Table 4.3).

Table 4.2   Women 60 and Over: Blacks Work Hard

	Race/Ethnicity				
	Asian	Black	Latino	White	Total
Almost All Blacks	9	42	21	33	106
Most Blacks	31	72	56	76	235
Some Blacks	54	51	99	88	292
Few Blacks	18	7	57	18	100
Almost No Blacks	3	1	13	4	21
Don't Know/Missing	30	26	44	53	153
Total	145	199	290	272	906

Table 4.3   Women 18–59: Blacks Work Hard

	Race/Ethnicity				
	Asian	Black	Latino	White	Total
Almost All Blacks	26	88	88	56	258
Most Blacks	56	162	131	136	485
Some Blacks	115	111	233	86	545
Few Blacks	37	11	80	9	137
Almost No Blacks	8	13	50	32	35
Don't Know/Missing	56	33	67	63	219
Total	298	405	624	352	1,679

To be specific, of the 447 Asian women queried, 39 percent ($n = 169$) responded "some blacks," 13.6 percent ($n = 58$) responded "few blacks," and 2.6 percent ($n = 11$) responded "almost no blacks."[1] Among Hispanic/Latina women, there were again less than positive views relayed, as 37 percent ($n = 333$) answered "some blacks," 15 percent ($n = 137$) answered "few blacks," and 4 percent ($n = 38$) answered "almost no blacks." Although slightly less negative, the trend continued among white women with close to 30 percent ($n = 174$) stating "some blacks," almost 5 percent ($n = 27$) stating "few blacks," and 1 percent ($n = 6$) stating "almost no blacks."

Survey participants were also asked if they perceive blacks as "easy to get along with" (see Tables 4.4 and 4.5). Seventy percent of whites conveyed generally positive perceptions with 176 stating "almost all blacks" and 242 stating "most blacks." There was some decrease among other the races and ethnicities within the subsample. Pointedly, slightly more than half of Hispanics/Latinos indicated that they found "almost all blacks" ($n = 223$) or "most blacks" ($n = 247$) as "easy to get along with." The decreasing trend continued among Asian women. Only 17 percent of Asian women ($n = 72$) noted that they find "almost all blacks easy to get along with" while 32 percent ($n = 138$) noted that "most blacks" are "easy to get along with."

Table 4.4   Women 60 and Over: "Blacks Easy to Get Along With"

| | Race/Ethnicity | | | | |
	Asian	Black	Latino	White	Total
Almost All Blacks	25	40	62	76	203
Most Blacks	46	70	76	91	283
Some Blacks	32	56	76	48	212
Few Blacks	12	6	20	9	47
Almost No Blacks	3	2	22	38	29
Don't Know/Missing	27	25	34	46	132
Total	145	199	290	272	906

Table 4.5   Women 18–59: "Blacks Easy to Get Along With"

| | Race/Ethnicity | | | | |
	Asian	Black	Latino	White	Total
Almost All Blacks	46	111	161	99	417
Most Blacks	90	134	171	150	545
Some Blacks	77	107	170	49	403
Few Blacks	21	18	52	4	35
Almost No Blacks	5	2	19	1	27
Don't Know/Missing	59	33	51	49	197
Total	298	405	624	352	1,679

Although the above queries were not directed toward or in relation to a specific black woman candidate, they provide unambiguous indications of how blacks are perceived by women of differing races and/or ethnicities. Such perceptions, likely reflections of prominent racial stereotypes, may impact their respective perceptions of a woman candidate who is also black. This is of particular interest, as women candidates are more likely to receive support from women voters (Smith and Fox 2001). Therefore, if black women candidates are likely to encounter stereotypical barriers among women voters as well, this potentially places them in a quandary as black women continue to pursue elected offices on the national level.

ANALYSIS: WOMEN, BLACK WOMEN, AND THE U.S. PRESIDENCY POST 2008

Once more, it was during the 2008 Democratic Primaries that most realized or acknowledged the unique position of black women in terms of candidate selection. Prior to the 2008 primaries, black women were simply seen as part of a larger racial group and therefore assumed likely to vote in accordance with that of the group's overall preference. It was not until the field of candidates whittled down to the three frontrunners—John Edwards, Hillary Clinton, and Barack Obama—did political scientists and media pundits take notice of the fact that black women's social location resides at the nexus of race and gender. Polls of likely voters were conducted in an attempt to perform more nuanced analyses and predict how black women would vote as the primary season progressed. Although initially torn, over time, black women soon began to support now President Barack Obama in droves in hopes of realizing a long-held of dreams of black Americans (see Chapter 3). The support of black women without a doubt helped now President Barack Obama to secure the U.S. Presidency.

Since the first election of Barack Obama to the U.S. Presidency, the lack of diversity within the national political arena remains at the forefront of public discourse considering the changing demographics of the U.S. population. The majority of high-ranking elected offices continue to be occupied by white males. As previously noted, although white women are increasingly occupying seats within both houses of the U.S. Congress, black women are largely underrepresented. For this reason, and specifically for the purposes of this analysis, additional data were collected approximately four years after the first election of President Barack Obama to the U.S. Presidency to explore the perceptions of race and gender in the context of state and national politics. Also, utilizing quantitative data, the self-perceived connectedness of black women to the state and federal governments was examined. Pointedly, like the focus groups highlighted in Chapter 3, respondents were asked about the future direction of the U.S. Presidency and Vice Presidency in the context of race and gender. The conduct of a quantitative study ultimately allowed for two tasks. First, comparative analyses by race, gender, and/or age group were made permissible. Secondly, because such analyses were permissible, tests of statistical significance using SPSS were also made possible. Hence, differences in perceptions by various demographic groupings were observed.[2] Questions that did not facilitate quantitative analyses were also included to allow for greater context and detail.

Questionnaire

The questionnaire employed to examine respondents' views of government in the context of race and gender contained a series of five-point Likert-scale items. Respondents were asked to strongly agree, agree, somewhat agree, disagree, or strongly disagree with the following statements.

- My issues are like other Americans.
- At some point, I have felt disconnected from the political process.
- I see people with whom I can identify on the national level.
- I will see a woman U.S, President in my lifetime.
- I will see a black woman U.S. President in my lifetime.

Results

In reporting the results, participants' responses were compared simply by gender regardless of race. Delving further, responses of those participants who self-identified as "female" were selected for more detailed analyses. Due to the smaller sample sizes of non-black races, the responses of women were categorized as "black" or "non-black" and compared accordingly.

Perceptions of Government: Women vs. Men

Taking a look at the sample's overall perceptions of government, women and men within the sample somewhat differed. Over 40 percent of women strongly agreed or agreed that their issues were like other Americans while only slightly more than 30 percent of males strongly agreed or agreed. However, more women (32 percent) than men (28 percent) indicated that they disagreed or strongly disagreed that their issues were like other Americans. Similarly, revealing a more than 20 point gap, over half of the women (54 percent) and slightly more than 30 percent of the men within the sample disagreed or strongly disagreed that elected and appointed members of government understand those issues important to them. Continuing in this fashion, close to 60 percent of women (59.4) and 46 percent of men disagreed or strongly disagreed that members of the government identify with them.

Moreover, 90 percent of women and 89 percent of men strongly agreed or agreed that a person's demographics impact their respective, lived experience. Participants were then asked to respond to questions regarding their perceptions of the potential impact of one's race and gender on the way in which they understand and/or interpret social and political issues. Again, there was division according to gender lines. While, there were similarities between the two genders in regard to one's demographics influencing their lived experiences, 86 percent of women and 70 percent of men strongly agreed or agreed that an elected official's personal demographics have an impact on how they perceive social and political issues. Thus, a smaller proportion of men agreed that one's demographics impact their interpretation of social and political issues.

When asked if there is an adequate number of women serving within the political arena on all levels of government, gender divisions once again emerged. Close to three-quarters (72 percent) of women disagreed or strongly disagreed with this statement, and exactly half of men disagreed or strongly disagreed with this statement. Probing into gender representation on the national level specifically, slightly more than 70 percent of women disagreed or strongly disagreed that there is an adequate number of women currently serving in elected offices. Precipitously lower, slightly less than half of men (49 percent) disagreed or strongly disagreed with this statement.

Women's (Black and Non-Black) Perceptions
of National Politics and Government

Taking a more nuanced look at differences between black women and non-black women, there was very little divergence.[3] To be explicit, there was very little statistically significant difference in terms of women's perceptions of government represented within the sample. Both black women and non-black women were more likely to agree that their issues were similar to those of other Americans. Black and non-black women also held similar perceptions of elected government officials, as both groups were more likely to disagree with the notion that members of government identify with them. Therefore, it was of little surprise that both groups indicated that they disagreed with the notion that there is an adequate number of women represented within the national political arena.

However, when asked explicitly about the possibility of seeing a woman U.S. President in their lifetime, there were statistically significant ($p < .05$)

differences detected. Black women, on average, responded that they agree that they will see a woman elected to the U.S. Presidency in their respective lifetimes while non-black women seemingly exhibited a greater sense of optimism either agreeing, and even strongly agreeing, with the notion of a woman within the Oval Office. When subsequently asked if they will ever see a *black* woman elected to the U.S. Presidency in their lifetime, black women were more likely, on average, to somewhat disagree with the statement. Non-black women, on average, were more likely to agree or somewhat agree with the statement. Although the differences regarding a black woman being elected to the U.S. Presidency were noticeable, the variations were not statistically significant ($p = .073$) but neared the .05 threshold.

Black and non-black women who self-identified as age 59 or younger were more likely to say that they agreed or strongly agreed, on average, that they will see a woman elected to the U.S. Presidency in their lifetime. However, those who self-identified as age 60 and over were more likely to disagree. Responses between and among age groups did not vary on a statistically significant basis, however. Yet, when asked about a *black* woman being elected to the U.S. Presidency, statistically significant variations surfaced. Statistics revealed that as the age of the respondents' increased, so did their likelihood to disagree or strongly disagree that they will see a black woman elected to the U.S. Presidency in their respective lifetimes ($p = .035$).

Black Women's Perceptions of Government and the U.S. Presidency

The vast majority of black women agreed or strongly agreed (87 percent) that one's race and gender have an influence on the way in which they perceive social and political issues. Furthermore, the majority of black women within the sample disagreed or strongly disagreed that members of the government do not identify with them as citizens (60 percent) or understand those issues pertinent to them (54 percent). In keeping with that trend, close to 63 percent of black women agreed or strongly agreed that members of national government have not addressed those issues pertinent to them. Ironically, 68 percent of black women stated that they do not, however, feel disconnected from the political process.

Probing their perceptions of the U.S. Presidency precisely, 66 percent of black women within the sample replied that they agree or strongly agree that they will see a woman elected to the U.S. Presidency. Conversely, when inquired about a black woman serving in the U.S. Presidency, there was a sharp decrease in the proportion of those who agreed or strongly agreed. In total, only 36 percent of black woman said that they agree or strongly agree that they will see a black woman elected to the U.S. Presidency in their lifetime. A comparison of means revealed statistical significance ($p = .000$) regarding black women's differing perceptions of seeing a women *versus* a black woman elected to the presidency. Just as highlighted in the above discussion, an examination by age groups found a statistically significant difference between those 18–20 years of age versus those 60 years of age and older. Those in the younger age group were more inclined to reply that they will see a black woman elected to the U.S. Presidency versus older black women in the sample ($p = .012$).

OPEN-ENDED RESPONSES

Women in the National Political Arena

Responses to open-ended questions provided greater insight into survey participants' views on the impact of gender and/or race within the national political arena. In general, survey participants' responses also mirrored those of previously published studies that have probed the lack of proportionate gender representation in national politics. Above all, the one theme that emerged among open-ended responses pertained to the perception of women in general as the "weaker" and more emotional sex. A multitude of female survey participants opined that, because of prevailing views of women as nurturers and emotional beings, many members of the general citizenry find it difficult to perceive women as leaders who are capable of maintaining objectivity in high-pressure situations. One female participant noted, for example, "women have always been viewed as inferior and weak in a sense (in comparison) to men, so the main barrier (to proportionate representation) is just the stereotype and the way women have been viewed in general." Another female participant succinctly reiterated, ". . . men think that women cannot handle the stress that will be demanded of [us]."

Although a vast majority of men acknowledged the stereotypes imposed on women seeking leadership positions, very few agreed with the notions of women being unable to handle leadership positions. For instance, one male participant explained,

Nobody believes that "a woman's place is in the home," but I think there's still an underlying set of double standards for women in our society. A woman running for office is still, to a degree, seen as different or exceptional—and not always in a good way. Despite extensive equality regulations, government is still male-oriented and male-dominated. This environment may still be somewhat reluctant to accept female lawmakers, executives, judges, etc.

Even still, there were one or two men that upheld the view that women are too emotional to hold leadership offices. As one male participant overtly stated, "I believe we consider the emotional aspect of women. I believe that the government is scared of letting a woman hold a strong amount of power because women [can become] emotional and it might negatively affect a situation."

Another theme that emerged among survey participants in regard to women seeking nationally elected offices is the lack of social networks necessary to garner the support necessary for a successful campaign. One female participant described the political arena as a "good ole boy" network that contends "women are not intellectually or emotionally capable [of political leadership]." Another female participant described the same barrier in the statement, "although a woman may have the credentials . . . politics is primarily an 'an all boys club' that allows women in their circle ever so often . . . they make an effort to not promote women as they would a man." A couple of male participants agreed with one writing, "raising money for campaigns is very problematic for many women who lack the network for financial backers." A female participant also identified social networks as a barrier to proportionate gender representation. Mirroring the findings generated by the recent study conducted by Fox and Lawless, the participant explained how networks and other social systems or institutions begin conditioning, and even encouraging, boys more so than girls to consider political office at an early age.

One respondent also noted the manner in which women candidates are expected to bear a greater burden than male candidates in respect to family obligations:

> On the superficial level, there are plenty of people who do not believe that women are capable of holding leadership positions. Systematically, boys and men continue to be groomed for leadership positions in ways that girls and women are not. Culturally, qualities that are valued in leaders are viewed positively in men, but negatively in women. (For instance, Hillary Rodham Clinton is often thought of as bitchy.) There is also the issue of work and family—women continue to shoulder many of the burdens of managing family life, which makes taking an active role in politics that much more difficult. For example, Sarah Palin and Rick Santorum both had young children with developmental disabilities at home, but Palin received much more criticism (from all parts of the political spectrum) for spending so much time away from her children.

Needless to say, the participant's identification of multiple barriers to the national political arena grounded in gender stereotypes and traditional gender roles indicates a reciprocating and interlocking system of marginalization functioning within and on the periphery of the political sphere.

Black Women and the National Political Arena

Focusing solely on black women, respondents also identified barriers related to the cumulative effects of race and gender in regard to entering the political arena. As evidenced above, when singularly referencing gender, most survey participants ascribed the stereotype of "weak" to women as a barrier to national political leadership. Ironically, when referencing the issue of race and gender, and in the context of black women pointedly, survey participants indicated that "aggressive" stereotypes beleaguer the general perception of black women. One female participant noted that, "(barriers to the national political arena exist) due to how black women in America are perceived. Many view black women as angry, hostile, aggressive individuals." Several female participants attributed pervading negative stereotypes to the media's portrayal of black women with one participant stating, "The media portrays black women as ghetto, disagreeable, crazy, and highly emotional."

Like the female respondents who stated that the nurturer stereotype served as a barrier to women's entry into the national political arena, a couple of male survey participants indicated that, the lack of black female representation in the political arena can be attributed to society's perceptions of the black woman's "role in American society as nurturer, black male supporter, and healer." Similarly, another male participant contended, "[it] is because black women used to do the most important job in America, mother our children. Since mothers have gone outside [of] the home, America has rapidly slipped into depravity." That both respondents were black potentially speaks to the ongoing sexism within the black community despite the contributions historically made by black women to the advance the black community as a whole (Robnett and Bany 2011). Moreover, one could, and with very little effort, argue that such statements perpetuates the "mammy" stereotype often attached to black women, that undoubtedly undermines the perception of black women as leaders, and in due course, the political aspirations of black women on a large scale (Hill-Collins 2000).

Just as survey participants noted networks as a barrier to proportionate gender representation, they indicated that this is especially true for black women. Some participants described the national political arena as a network within itself that works to "limit the influence of African-American men and women in politics." Another participant explained that such networks are sustained, and blacks thus excluded from national political offices, "mostly because the people in office have a direct connection to people in office [i.e., they are a family or friend relation]. If we would elect people who are really qualified, we would see some diversity in office." An example of this exclusion was provided by a separate, black female respondent who shared her experience in trying to enter the political arena.

It's all about who you know. For example, I have tried to get a position on Capitol Hill for a few years, and each time it seems the [minimum qualifications] increases . . . The general public knows that if you have a personal affiliation with the people on the Hill, the chances of you getting employed is highly likely especially if you are [a son or daughter of one of] them.

Several respondents acknowledged the historical aspects of race and gender within the national arena as long-standing barriers. As one female respondent pointed out, ". . . the government was created and designed to govern the lives of the people of this country. Women, during the time of its creation, were unable to vote. (Women) have since been given a few rights and have made some strides. But the government is still run by men with an agenda to suit their needs." Likewise, taking race into consideration, one participant commented, "race and gender still matter in the ole US of A . . . the legacy of the past still influences how far blacks and women have (to go) compared to white men today."

CONCLUSION

"Founding Fathers," a term used with endearment to describe those who established this country, also underscores the innately patriarchal nature of this country's origin. From this country's very inception, the government was established to be managed by those whose demographics classify them as both male and white. Written by a group of white males, the very document designed to establish, guide, and ensure the perpetuity of this nation overtly refers to males as the leaders of this country. Because of the ongoing sexism that has become institutionalized in the political sphere, women must persist in challenging traditional gender norms that prevent their entry into the national political arena.

It is clear that, through the lenses of those who drafted and ratified the document, this country was only to be led by those who look like them. Therefore, it is no surprise that, at one point in time, African slaves and their descendants were not even acknowledged as being whole human beings. Fast forward to the twenty-first century, and much has changed. Still, at the risk of sounding like an old cliché, much has remained the same. Although the country elected its first African-American male to serve in the U.S. Presidency, it was done so many decades after the ratification of the 13th, 14th, and 15th amendments which freed and granted citizenship and the right to vote to African slaves. Not to mention, events preceding and following the election of Barack Obama in and of itself, shed light on the continued racism still prevalent in this country. As previously noted, politicians of color must still contend with racialized stereotypes that still pervade U.S. social and political institutions. As the United States has just elected its first black president, and has yet to elect a female to the U.S. Presidency, a woman of color seeking to become Commander-in-Chief must overcome both racism and sexism deeply ingrained within the fiber of the political sphere and the general population. Survey results reveal that although a woman being elected to the U.S. Presidency is foreseeable by survey participants, a black woman as the U.S. President is not. Thus, the introduction of race in conjunction with gender serves as a barrier. In looking at the responses of women participants within the 2008 CMPS, a greater proportion of black women (34 percent), in comparison to Asian (23 percent), Latina (18 percent), and white (16 percent) women, indicated that they believe people of their respective race downplay their racial identity. Undoubtedly, this is done to mitigate stereotypes and encourage acceptance by others due to the historical and ongoing treatment of blacks in this country on a both de facto and de jure basis.

Through the lenses of those who stand at the nexus of race and gender, the national political sphere is one that is not inclusive of them. As illustrated via survey results, black women within the study sample do not perceive members of the national political arena as understanding of those issues that directly impact them. Black women within the sample also failed to see many in the political arena with whom they could identify. Despite the fact that they do not perceive their issues as being addressed on the national level, the majority of black women within the sample indicated that they do not feel disconnected from the political process. Perhaps, because they do not perceive their issues as being addressed, black women remain connected to the process in order to advocate for themselves and their communities. In comparison to their female counterparts of other races and ethnicities, black women were more inclined to engage in the democratic process (see Table 4.6). Of note, results from the 2008 CMPS revealed that a greater proportion of black women volunteered on a political campaign.

Nonetheless, regardless of their demonstrated connectedness to the political process, women of color remain underrepresented within the national political arena. Stereotypes as well as systemically reinforced inequalities facilitate the underrepresentation. Although women of all races and ethnicities, in and outside of the national political arena, must deal with traditional

Table 4.6 Women's Volunteer Political Participation by Race

| | Worked as Volunteer | | |
	Yes	No	Total
Asian	44	397	915
Black	125	479	441
Latino	93	822	604
White	80	545	625
	342	2,243	2,594

gender norms, black women must also contend with the dual oppressions of race and gender. As identified in open-ended survey responses, institutions such as the media serve to reiterate negative stereotypes of black women, undermining society's ability to perceive them as objective, level-headed leaders. In addition, social and professional networks remain closed off to historically marginalized groups, including black women, placing them at a disadvantage in terms of garnering support needed to launch an extensive, national campaign. Yet, analyses reveal that younger women, both black and non-black, believe they will see a black woman U.S. President in their lifetime. Subsequent chapters will probe the roles of social networks, media and the changing U.S demography.

NOTES

1. Sixty-six responded "don't know" and 20 refused to respond.

2. Employing a convenience sampling method, an electronic link to the survey was distributed via email. To expand the sample, survey respondents originally in receipt of the email containing a link to the survey were also invited to share the link with other persons potentially interested in sharing their views. In total, 282 persons completed the survey. Thirty-four of those questionnaires were omitted due to missing values or indicating an age less than 18. Ultimately, the final sample was comprised of 251 persons. Because the survey was a continuation of the qualitative data collection effort presented in Chapter 3, black women were purposefully oversampled ($n = 132$). For comparison purposes, men and women belonging to other races and ethnicities ($n = 119$) were also invited to complete the survey to potentially ascertain the extent to which the perceptions of black women regarding race and gender representation, if at all, differed from those demographically different. As such, in addition to African-American/black men ($n = 49$), the final sample also included a smaller number of persons who also self-identified as American Indian/Alaska Native ($n = 3$), Asian/Pacific Islander ($n = 17$), Hispanic/Latino ($n = 11$), and white ($n = 39$).

3. Due to the low number of American Indians/Alaska Natives present in the sample, significance values could not be calculated.

Chapter 5

The Impact of the Media's Portrayal of Black Women

For most persons, the media is the primary method through which information is accessed. Consequently, as a social institution, the media plays an integral role in shaping cultural perceptions and norms (Adoni and Mane 1984). In doing so, the media has great influence on the ways in which people utilize information to navigate social and personal interactions and processes (Garfield 2007; Abraham and Appiah 2006; Eschholz and Gertz 2003; Berger 2000). This is especially true for those who may be socially distant from a specific topic or issue (Adoni and Mane 1984). In this case, the media becomes the sole source of information, reifying their influence over the manner in which a topic, issue, and/or phenomenon may be interpreted by the larger public (Gargield 2007; Klein 2003; Iyengar 1989; Gerbner, Morgan, and Signorielli 1982).

Because of the significant influence the media has over the constantly evolving, yet prevailing, norms and perceptions, a tremendous amount of research and scholarship has been conducted and produced respectively. Expressly, scholars from a range of fields including communication, the social and political sciences, and so on, have examined the influence of the media on public perceptions, and thus, social processes (Eschholz and Gertiz 2003; Berger 2000; Adoni and Mane 1984). Such studies consistently reaffirm the notion that, while the media is a purveyor of vital information and facts, it also is expert at creating a subjective reality that seemingly perpetuates a status quo that upholds the socially manufactured hierarchy. The simultaneous and convergent use of symbols, visual imagery, and social rhetoric by media outlets advances and supports the social hierarchy in which sexism and racism work independently and in tandem to marginalize women, and more specifically as will be examined, women of color (Callahan 2012; Carptenter 2012; Black and Peacock 2011; Bjornstrom et al. 2010; Abraham and Appiah 2006; deCoteau, Jamieson, and Rober 1998; Adoni and Mane 1984).

MEDIA'S DEPICTION OF WOMEN

The issue of women in the media has long been a controversial one. More specifically, the issue of sexism in the media has been one of controversy and angst. Feminist scholars have, for many years, contended that the overall depiction of women in the media furthers stereotypes traditionally associated with women (Posavac, Posavac, and Posavac 1998). Of those stereotypes, women are typically illustrated as helpless, intellectually inferior, beauty products and fashion obsessed, and in a constant state of yearning for the perfect, lifelong mate. Among the more widely recognized gender-related disparities represented within and by the media is the sexual objectification of women. On a disproportionate scale, commercials, television shows, music videos, and films all portray women in settings or modes that suggest or invoke erotic notions among viewers. Such efforts or actions on the part of the media convey that women are for the superficial purposes of viewing pleasure and must therefore be appeasing to their respective viewing audiences. At the other end of the spectrum, however, the media has traditionally portrayed women as the virtuous, loving, and supportive mother and role model. Media characterizations of women as being supportive of their families and loved ones have facilitated the generally accepted view of women as nurturers and caregivers. From the initial emergence of television to present day, sitcoms and dramas have frequently portrayed women as the domestic mainstay and core support unit of the family (e.g., June Cleaver on *Leave It to Beaver*, Marion Cunningham on *Happy Days*, Elyse Keaton on *Family Ties*, Carol Brady on the *Brady Bunch*, etc.).

Due to the above stereotypes, women, widely perceived as having little substance or expert knowledge to contribute, have encountered many difficulties within professional settings. In fact, for numerous years, women were often relegated to the role of secretary or a similar position to simply support the professional agendas or activities of male executives. It has only been in the last 20 plus years that women have begun to *increasingly* occupy professional or managerial positions (Bureau of Labor Statistics 2014; Wozencraft 2001). Gender stereotypes, nonetheless, continue to beleaguer the progress made by women within the professional realm. For female politicians, the media remains a considerable challenge.

Women Politicians and the Media

In conjunction with the historically customary practice of promoting or selecting men for leadership roles in and outside of the political arena, the consistent placement or consignment of women in supportive television and film roles has made the national political arena a difficult one for women to enter. Just as the media once portrayed women in solely supportive scripted roles, the media has also played a quite influential role in crafting how female candidates are received by voters (Falk 2010). As a culture that now, and on a non-ending basis, surveils and documents actions, interactions, conversations, verbal statements, and the likes on social media sites, the media now plays a very fundamental role in voter's perceptions of political issues and candidates (Falk 2010; Schlehofer et al. 2011). The media, it can be argued, is *the* primary source from which members of the general citizenry access any and all information regarding political candidates. Thus, it can also be argued that the manner in which the media frame a political candidate may make or break a candidate's bid for elected office. As a result, politicians and political candidates are often vigilant about their words and actions in order to prevent what could become a hindrance to a successful campaign, or even a career-ending scandal, in the era of the 24/7 news cycle. As a consequence, when women make the decision to pursue political office, they also make the decision to place themselves under heavy scrutiny by the media. Granted, male candidates are also placed under scrutiny by the media. However, it is widely agreed that women politicians must contend with a double standard—one that requires them to exhibit strong leadership skills coupled with compassion and warmth (Gershon 2012; Falk 2010). Upon entering the political arena, and the national political arena distinctively, female politicians of present day enter what can only be described as a vortex comprised of 24/7 cable news channels, twenty-first century social media applications and sites, and traditional gender norms, quite frequently, propagated by the media. Multiple studies have examined the role of the media in influencing voter perceptions and have consistently demonstrated that media outlets are more likely to impose traditional gender roles on to female candidates via cues and implicit messages (Gershon 2012; Schlehofer 2011; Robertson et al. 1999).

Empirical evidence reveals that the media often exhibit gender biased when covering political campaigns involving candidates of both genders (Gershon 2012; Schlehofer 2011; Robertson et al. 1999). The most obvious demonstration of gender bias by media outlets is the constant acknowledgement of female candidates' gender. According to Eargle, Esmail, and Sullivan, media outlets, in the course of their respective political coverage, are more likely to point out the gender of women candidates (2008). Less obvious expressions of gender bias among media outlets have been detected in the verbal cues employed to describe politicians. Several studies have demonstrated that, when a woman candidate is running for a political office, her leadership qualities are explicitly highlighted while the leadership skills of male candidates are rarely, if ever, mentioned (Bystrom et al. 2001; Kahn 1996). Such verbal cues on the part of the media impart to voters that the leadership skills of males are innate, and therefore, do not require articulated recognition. In addition, due to the aforementioned traditional gender roles, women candidates are also expected to adhere the social needs of the constituency as a demonstration of the warmth and compassion presumed on the part of female candidates (Schlehofer 2011; Robertson et al. 1999; Carroll and Schreiber 1997). In accordance with a brief discussion in Chapter 4, media outlets are more inclined to focus on gender-specific issues when the candidate is female versus when a candidate is male. Hence, when women focus on those issues that are largely perceived as "male issues," including defense and the economy, then they are portrayed and subsequently perceived as attempting to be masculine resulting in poor reception among the voter population (Falk 2010). However, when women are portrayed as focusing on "women's issues" such as child care, education, health care, they are then portrayed and perceived as competent by the media (Falk 2010). To do otherwise may be perceived as a divergence from traditional roles and result in voters' condemnation.

In comparison to male candidates, female candidates are also expected to conform to the hegemonic ideals of femininity and beauty often imposed on women in general. As previously discussed, preferred images of beauty permeate media outlets reifying how women must look and present themselves in order to be accepted by the vast majority of the public (Posavac, Posavac, and Wiegel 2001; Posavac, Posavac, and Posavac 1998). Due to the dominating images of attractiveness and beauty, women politicians are also expected to reflect such images despite seeking leadership offices that are more inclined to require an individual or executive with critical thinking and adept crisis management skills. For this reason, media outlets and pundits are not above commenting on the wardrobe and fashion choices of female politicians, again, holding them to a different standard than that of male candidates.

Of note, during the 2008 Democratic primaries, unlike male candidates, the wardrobe of presidential candidate Hillary Clinton was often the subject of many media pundit discussions for appearing too manly or gender neutral (Bratskeir 2009). On those occasions when she has deviated from her usually conservative attire, media outlets have also focused resources and time to covering her wardrobe change as if it is germane to the country's governance (Moss 2009; Wheaton 2007). Aside from media pundits and the general citizenry, former Secretary of State and U.S. Senator Clinton was the target of what has been deemed a sexist and irrelevant comment about her wardrobe choice during a nationally televised presidential debate. Former U.S. Senator and presidential candidate John Edwards opted to take time from debating actual issues in order to comment, "I admire what Senator Clinton has done for America, what her husband did for America . . . [but] um, I'm not sure about that coat." The decision by former Senator Edwards to mock then presidential candidate Clinton's attire during a national debate not only took attention away from the issues that actually impact the day-to-day experiences of American individuals and families, it also obliquely underscored his opponent's gender, and in doing so, attempted to reframe the general public's perceptions of her as a leader (Andrews 2007).

Oddly, although then presidential candidate never dressed in manner that could be deemed unprofessional, media and political experts were often focused on whether her attire made her appear too feminine or too masculine as likely proxies for their perceived assessment of her weakness or strength as a political candidate and potential Commander in Chief. At one point in the primaries, Clinton began to cry in an open forum while expressing her feelings about the pressures of campaigning on a national stage. Needless to say, the event became a topic for fodder and once again focused on the topic of gender in politics.

Historical and Current Depictions of Black Women in the Media

To confound matters, the media has repeatedly set forth what it perceives as the ideal woman—one who is tall, thin, and physically attractive (Posavac, Posavac, and Weigel 2001; Posavac, Posavac, and Posavac 1998; Heinberg and Thompson 1995; Cash and Henry 1985). Of course, it should be noted that attractiveness is most often, though not always, symbolized or represented among media outlets and products as someone who often has long, flowing hair and more often than not, is white effectively reinforcing hegemonic ideals of beauty, and more importantly, general acceptability and likeability. Accordingly, since the media has used such an ideal type in a range of media products including advertisements, news programming, films, and television series, a dichotomy has been created and propagated among the general citizenry. As part of this carefully crafted dichotomy, the "norm" is that which precisely or closely reflects the symbolic representation of attractiveness and likeability, and the "other" is that which does not (i.e., such hegemonic representations may be seen in celebrities that dominate news and entertainment media including Jennifer Aniston, Tea Leoni, Kaley Cuoco, Scarlett Johansson, Charlize Theron, Mika Brzezinski, Katie Couric, Diane Sawyer, Brianna Keilar, etc.).

For decades, as the default "other," black women have been depicted in film and television in a range of roles that perpetuate long-standing yet ongoing stereotypes (Sewell 2013; Carpenter 2012; Harris-Perry 2011; Rousseau 2009; Smith-Shomade 2009; Abraham and Appiah 2006; Hill-Collins 2000). Despite the traditions and contributions of black women to their respective communities, rarely are black women portrayed as highly intelligent and reserved individuals who seek to contribute to the betterment of the collective, human condition. Typically, black women have been portrayed in myriad television shows and films as drug abusers, unfit mothers, loud, incompetent, confrontational, overly sexualized, and/or prostitutes (e.g., *Precious, Losing Isaiah, Poetic Justice, Hustle and Flow, Monster's Ball, Antwone Fisher, Get On Up, Ray, Friday, For Colored Girls*, various *In the Heat of the Night episodes*, etc.) (Sewell 2013; Carpenter 2012; Harris-Perry 2011; Rousseau 2009; Smith-Shomade 2003; Hill-Collins 2000). Such visual images perpetuate the prevailing notion that black women are immoral and corrupt, and hence, in no way suitable for high-ranking positions of authority.

Even more likable characters have served to perpetuate stereotypes of black women. A well-known example, *Gimme a Break!*'s Nell Carter was a highly talented and ambitious singer who gave up pursuing a promising music career in order to take care of her deceased friend's family. As the central character of the show, Nell spends all of her time cleaning, cooking, and caring for a white widower and his three daughters. Consequently, although Nell's character in no way reflected any of the above morally questionable characteristics or behaviors, her character still conformed to a historical stereotype that limits black women to a role of servitude for the benefit of the racial majority.

Though not as overt as it once was in the media, the mammy stereotype, as evidenced above, remains present in contemporary television (e.g., The Pine Sol lady, Louise in *Sex in the City*, Charlene in *Bringing Down the House*, etc.). The stereotype of the mammy seeks to portray a black woman, typically overweight, as one who is willing to sacrifice her own needs and wants in order to focus on the desires and necessities of whites. While doing so, she is generally hard working and happy. Because she rarely complains, she often becomes a confident and emotional burden bearer for those she serves. As delineated in *Black Feminist Thought*, the mammy stereotype was "created to justify the economic exploitation of house slaves and sustained to explain black women's long-standing restriction to domestic service, the mammy image represents the normative yardstick used to evaluate all black women's behavior" (Hill-Collins 2000). Thus, assuming an occupational role outside of that which reflects the mammy stereotype serves as a challenge to the hegemonic norms regarding black women's professional capabilities and skills.

As noted earlier, the media is often the medium through which people often access and/or negotiate reality, the media has a tremendous impact on overall population perceptions. Black feminist scholars have carefully, and in great detail, examined the role of media depictions and imagery on shaping and influencing the prevailing perceptions of black women by members of the general citizenry. In their respective scholarship, Hill-Collins, Harris-Perry, and hooks, to name a few, have delineated the manner in which stereotypes impact the lived experiences of black women. Once more, in her groundbreaking work, *Black Feminist Thought*, Hill-Collins discusses how ubiquitous media images of black women shape the belief systems of individuals regarding black women ultimately forcing black women to contend, counter, and challenge prevailing stereotypes that consistently reinforce notions of black women as the collective antithesis of morality and goodness. Despite the individual and collective contributions and sacrifices made by black women to uplift the marginalized, such images have effectively pervaded all sectors of society, including the political arena.

In present day, it should go without saying that the media maintain a constant and undeniable presence in all forms including television, film, print magazines, and as a home to countless news and entertainment digital outlets, the internet. Due to the ubiquitous nature of the internet, and social media outlets more importantly, members of the general citizenry are inundated with images of a range of media personalities on a non-stop basis. As a consequence, in addition to increasing the popularity of reality television shows, the social media via the internet has also played a pivotal role in converting the cast members of such shows into well-known individuals, if not in demand celebrities. Recent television shows such as the Real Housewives of Atlanta (RHOA) primarily include a cast of professional, well-accomplished black women. On the surface, the television show appears to be a progression for black women in television. However, the show, and others like it that include primarily black female cast members, often depict the stars of the show fighting (both verbally and physically), yelling, and back-biting perpetuating negative stereotypes of black women. Like RHOA, Basketball Wives also depicts wealthy black women often engaged in bickering and other negative behaviors stereotypically associated with black women. Needless to say, the antics of the cast members on the respective shows often captures the attention of the media which then dedicates a tremendous amount of effort and resources to further publicizing the behaviors of the cast members. Critics of both shows and others like it often contend that, what should be platforms to depict black women in a positive light, often fail to do so, and instead, does quite the opposite.

The Portrayal of Black Female Politicians in the Media

In 2008, Eargle, Ashraf, and Sullivan conducted a content analysis to determine if, and to what extent, media coverage varies according to candidates' demographics. Upon the conclusion of their analysis, study investigators detected variation according to candidates' respective race or gender. Those candidates who were not white males, Hillary Clinton and Barack Obama to be specific, were more likely to have their gender or race respectively highlighted by members of the media (Piston 2010). Then presidential candidate

Obama, it was noted by members of the media, avoided mentioning his race until he was forced to do so in his widely televised speech on race as a result of racially tinged events surrounding the 2008 presidential election. Then presidential candidate Obama's efforts to de-racialize himself is not uncommon among minority political candidates. As referenced in Chapter 4, black or African-American political candidates are often compelled to de-racialize themselves in an effort to disassociate themselves from stereotypes historically attributed to blacks (e.g., corrupt, lazy, unintelligent, unapproachable, etc.) (Weaver 2012; Piston 2010; Jeffries and Jones 2006; Jeffries 1999). For instance, as Jeffries revealed upon the conclusion of his analysis of Douglass Wilder's successful gubernatorial campaign, while Douglass Wilder received positive media coverage comparable to his opponent, he also received negative media coverage greater than that of his opponent. (Jefferies 1999). Consequently, like women in general, black women politicians must contend with the cumulative and reciprocating forces of the 24/7 news cycle, social media, and cultural norms grounded in gender. Unlike women in general, or white women specifically, black women politicians must also contend with the challenges associated with race.

Female candidates of color are also more likely to receive negative media coverage. In an online experimental study, Gershon demonstrated that, in comparison to white female candidates, black female candidates received less press coverage (2013). However, they did receive greater press coverage than Latina candidates. On the other hand, black female candidates were less likely than white female candidates to receive media coverage in relation to policy formulation or legislative agendas. However, black and Latina female candidates were more likely to receive press coverage in relation to corruption or political scandal (Gershon 2013). It should be noted that this is ironic, as Bystrom et al. concluded at the conclusion of their study focusing on gender bias in politics, that women candidates are typically framed as being more honest and compassionate than their male counterparts (2001). Again, the introduction of race in conjunction with gender appears to have a multiplicative effect that serves as a challenge to black female candidates within the media. As a result of black female candidates' framing by the media, it is no surprise that Philpot and Walton (2007) discovered that minority candidates are more likely to obtain voter support from other minority females, as females of color, as noted by Harris-Perry, are more likely to identify with and have empathy for black female candidates due to a shared collective history (2011).

Even still, black women remain steadfast in serving public offices. For a number of black women, serving in the national political arena has proven to be exigent, to say the least. Media framing of black women has often perpetuated notions of black women as unfit or unprepared for national office.

Though politicians on a whole experience media scrutiny, black women are disproportionately impacted by media coverage, and more importantly, skewed media framing.

Notable Examples of the Media and Black Women in the National Political Arena

In 1991, news reports leaked findings from a private interview conducted by the Federal Bureau of Investigation (FBI) with Anita Hill, a then unknown law professor, on her work experiences with then-Supreme Court nominee Clarence Thomas (Siegel 2011). At the time of the leak, the Senate Judiciary Committee was in the process of holding confirmation hearings of then nominee Clarence Thomas. It was assumed that the confirmation hearings would close with little, if any, objections or surprises. However, once Ms. Hill's interview with the FBI, during which she revealed multiple instances of sexual harassment by Thomas, was brought to light by media outlets, members of the Senate Judiciary Committee allowed her testimony regarding her statements. Widely televised live to millions worldwide, many have hailed it as the watershed moment in exposing pervasive sexual harassment in the American workplace. Equally so, many were unsettled, and even infuriated, by the way in which Anita Hill was verbally derided by various persons including high-ranking government officials via the media (Siegel 2011; Suro 1999). Ms. Hill's statements regarding the sexual harassment she ensured while employed as Mr. Thomas' assistant were met with visceral opposition and accusations of her misleading, if not outright lying, to the FBI and members of the Senate Judiciary Committee. Simply stated, Ms. Hill's character and integrity were questioned and attacked.

Unfortunately, Professor Hill was simply one of the first in a series of accomplished black women whose integrity and competence have been vilified under the scope of the media. Another now well-known legal scholar was also ensnared by a perfect storm of media scrutiny and national politics. Two years after Professor Hill's unplanned foray into national politics, Lani Guinier, a graduate of Yale Law School, was nominated by then President Clinton to serve as the Attorney General for Civil Rights within the United States Department of Justice. Then President Clinton knew Ms. Guinier as a law school classmate, but had never opted to read her scholarship regarding voting rights. Specifically, Ms. Guinier was the author of multiple papers that proposed what was deemed a "radical" system of voting in an attempt to ameliorate disenfranchisement among members of the African-American community who had expressed discontentment with their political voices being heard by the overall political structure (Levine 1993). Not very long after her publications were discovered and read by members of the media, President

Clinton's political opposition, U.S. Congressional Republicans precisely, labeled Ms. Guinier as a "quota queen" and exclaimed her political views as racist and illogical (Levine 1993). To compound matters, the same man who nominated her, withdrew her name from further consideration without allowing her to explain writings to members of the congressional confirmation committee. Reflecting on her experience months later, Ms. Guinier stated that she felt vilified by members of the media who she said allowed then President Clinton's political opponents to frame and distort her scholarship and legal ideas.

In an eerily similar fashion, in 2013, President Obama nominated then U.N. Ambassador Susan Rice to serve as U.S. Secretary of State subsequent to the announcement by then U.S. Secretary of State Hillary Clinton that she planned to resign the post. During the latter part of then Secretary Clinton's tenure at the State Department, the U.S. Embassy in Benghazi, Libya, was attacked by Islamic extremists. Two American citizens were killed in the course of the attacks. Ambassador Rice, a graduate of both Stanford and Oxford Universities, soon became the target of President Obama's political opposition, who questioned and implicated her in the Benghazi tragedy. Due to then Secretary Clinton's unavailability, then U.N. Ambassador Rice appeared on several talk shows in her stead to discuss the Benghazi incident in addition to other topics pertaining to international relations. While answering questions specific to the Benghazi incident, Ambassador Rice utilized information that had been provided to her by U.S. intelligence entities. In response to her televised interviews, Congressional Republicans utilized media outlets to openly and overtly accuse her of misleading the American citizenry and characterize her as unfit for the position of U.S. Secretary of State. Although she continued to garner support from President Obama, as a consequence of the constant media scrutiny, Ambassador Rice soon thereafter withdrew her name from further consideration for U.S. Secretary of State.

As a politician's wife, and therefore a magnet for indefatigable media attention, the First Lady of the United States must often endure both praise and criticism. Historically, first ladies have been frequently critiqued on their attire, hair, and/or interactions with the general public. Moreover, historically, all of the first ladies have all had one thing in common—race. Hence, the seminal U.S. Presidential campaign, and subsequent of election, of Barack Obama broke the long-lasting trend of white women as First Lady of the United States. As previously indicated in Chapter 3, focus group participants described Mrs. Obama as being skilled and intelligent. Thus not surprisingly, the image of an African-American woman as the First Lady has filled many African-American women with an enormous sense of pride and admiration. In the last two years, she has regularly appeared on the front page of several magazines. It is not uncommon to overhear African-American women in public spaces describe Mrs. Obama as intelligent, beautiful, accomplished, well-dressed, and so on. She has also been described as a woman who has proven that you can have it all (i.e., career, husband, children, etc.). Accordingly, she has become a role model for many African-Americans—both young and old.

Even so, the media's reaction to Mrs. Obama has been, and continues to be, one of fascination, anticipation, and, at times, outright political incorrectness. As mentioned in Chapter 3, it was during the 2008 U.S. presidential election season when Mrs. Obama stated that, for the first time in her life as an adult, she was proud of her country (CBS News 2008). In the media's ensuing in-depth questioning of the meaning or catalyst behind Mrs. Obama's statements, as a collective, it failed to seize an opportunity for what could have been a teachable moment for many outside of the African-American community. Within the African-American community, there was no question regarding the impetus of her statements. For the many African-Americans who are acutely aware of the history of racism and continued disparities in this country, it was a welcomed affirmation. Though Mrs. Obama's statements surrounded her excitement for the increase in the number of people of all races becoming civically engaged, the number of African-Americans who registered to vote, and subsequently did so, reached record numbers (Alex-Assensoh 2008; Walters 2008). Prior to President Obama's candidacy, because of the legacies of de jure racism and systemic inequality, many African-Americans did not believe they would live to see an African-American president. Thus, witnessing the support for and election of the first African-American president likely spurred those in the African-American community who had once been somewhat apathetic regarding politics and the voting process. Once more, this was the sentiment of focus group participants who commented that minority participation in politics may increase as a result of Obama's successful campaign. Nevertheless, mainstream media overlooked the historical genesis of Mrs. Obama's statements, and therefore, the chance to gain greater insight into the African-American community's perceptions of the political process in the context of African-Americans' experience in American history. In fact, one major media outlet, *The New Yorker*, literally chose to portray Mrs. Obama as a gun-toting radical on the cover of its July 21, 2008, issue. The actions on behalf of the media, and *The New Yorker* precisely, were rather surprising, as Mrs. Clinton often engaged in health care policy matters much to the chagrin of many members of Congress. While serving in the role of First Lady of the United States, Mrs. Clinton spearheaded a widely publicized and debated effort to overhaul health care in the United States. Because of her actions, she was often described as overstepping her role as the First Lady. Yet, unlike Mrs. Obama, Mrs. Clinton was never visually or illustratively displayed in a disparaging manner (see one of many *Time Magazine* covers).

After clarifying her statements on more than one instance, Mrs. Obama made it clear to the American public that her primary role at the White House would be as "Mom-In-Chief" (Gibbs 2009; Puente 2008). Mrs. Obama took painstaking efforts to emphasize that she would not be involved in the creation of policy, instead focusing on her two daughters. Similarly, Mrs. Obama made it clear that her time in the White House would also include focusing on the families of military personnel (Ruggeri 2009; Samuels 2009).

It seems as though Mrs. Obama has been quite welcomed in this role, as she has been complimented on her ability to communicate and identify with military wives and children. Although, she has made a couple of public appearances to speak in support of President Obama's policy agenda, she has maintained her focus on her children and the families of military personnel. When she has made public comments in support of President Obama's policy agenda, there was a show of concern by individuals stating that they wanted her to maintain her role as "Mom-In-Chief" (Swarns 2009). Consequently, one must ask if the public's acceptance and comfort with Mrs. Obama as "Mom-In-Chief" is reflective of society's stereotypical perceptions and perpetuations of black women as "caregivers" (Harris-Perry 2011; Hill-Collins 2000). After all, when looking at Dr. Jill Biden, there seems to be some variance in the way in which society has responded to her works and activities versus that of Mrs. Obama since the 2008 presidential election. In 2010, at the request of President Obama, Dr. Biden coordinated and hosted a community college conference to help define the role of community colleges in the Obama administration (Jones 2010; Office of the White House Press Secretary 2010). This is not too surprising considering Dr. Biden teaches at Northern Virginia Community College as she did at Delaware Technical and Community College prior to the election of her husband as second in command. Ironically, there was no push back from the general citizenry via the media regarding Dr. Biden's decision to continue pursuing her professional aspirations independently or within the context of the policy agenda of the White House.

It should be acknowledged that the above discussed examples were not women actively seeking an elected office. Still, their respective experiences under the intense spotlight of the media provides perspective, and as a result, understanding of the tenuous relationship between black women within the national political arena and the media. As a result, those black women who actively seek or are interested in a national political office must contend with the negative images surrounding black women within the national political sphere. As evidenced by the experiences of Maxine Waters, for example, those black women who have been elected to an office within or connected to the national political arena have also endured media coverage that has questioned their integrity and painted them in a less than positive light.

First elected to the U.S. Congress in 1991, U.S. Representative Waters has played a pivotal role in ensuring civil rights within the United States and abroad (Robinson, 1999). In spite of her contributions to the U.S. House of Representatives, U.S. Representative Waters, in addition to other members of the Congressional Black Caucus, became the subjects of investigative inquiry by the Office of Congressional Ethics (OCE), a congressional entity established shortly after the election of President Obama to his first term. According to the OCE, Representative Waters misused her influence in an attempt to funnel money to a bank where her husband held investments. In response, the media covered the investigation on multiple occasions emphasizing potential inappropriate behavior on her part (Condon 2010; Margasak 2010; CBS 2010). The investigations carried on for more than two years and failed to prove that Representative Waters engaged in any financial impropriety on her part. Despite not having any proven evidence of wrongdoing on the part of Representative Waters, the media's unrelenting coverage and framing of the events, appear to have served, to a degree, as inspiration to an episode of the CBS police drama, *Blue Bloods,* that aired at approximately the same time as the OCE initiated its investigations and the media firestorm commenced. On the episode, which aired on November 19, 2010, a black councilwoman is accused of misappropriating local government funds to take trips out of the country. Such media framing and skewed depictions relay, or further perpetuate, the image of black women as untrustworthy, and therefore unsuitable for public office.

INTERVIEWS WITH PROFESSIONAL BLACK WOMEN

Since the establishment of slavery, African-American women have always been vulnerable to discriminatory actions within the U.S. labor market (Edghill 2007). Of note, during World War I, African-American women were often not considered first for positions in war plants. Further, despite being qualified, African-American women were denied access to lower level clerical positions that emerged upon the ending of the World War I. Because of this, they were compelled to accept positions for which they were overqualified included cleaning and doing laundry. Due to the Civil Rights Act and other employment laws, African-American women were able to enter white-collar sectors toward the end of the twentieth century (Edghill 2007). However, lower pay, in comparison to their white male and female counterparts, persisted for African-American women (Edghill 2007). In 2000, it was concluded, that toward the end of the twentieth century, white women were promoted to higher paying positions at a considerably higher rate than their African-American female counterparts (Conrad 2005).

Immediately following the first election of Barack Obama to the U.S. Presidency, informal, one-on-one discussions with professional black women of varying ages and occupations regarding President Obama's cabinet appointments, of which were multiple women of color, revealed anecdotal evidence suggesting that, although black women are increasingly obtaining postsecondary degrees and occupying professional positions, enduring the cumulative effects of race and gender are often the norm. Despite reports of commercial success enjoyed by women of color of late, when talking with professional black women, it was not uncommon for "war stories" regarding their respective employers that point to racism and/or sexism to emerge. These stories often entailed inappropriate comments such as, "you're going to be our diversity monkey" or the well-known "you speak so well." Inappropriate comments mentioned also included, "you two look just alike" to pairs of minority women who look nothing alike. Moreover, stories entailed the underutilization of skills (i.e., asking minority women with advanced degrees to make copies, travel arrangements, etc.). Without fail, in an exasperated tone, each conversation ended with the same comment or similar tone each time—"they just don't know what to do with us."

Nonetheless, one could argue that such discussions immediately following the election of the first African-American U.S. President was somewhat premature, as an adequate amount of time had not passed to truly gauge the impact of his election on the lived experiences of professional black women within the workplace. More specifically, not enough time had passed to determine the impact, if any, was perceived by professional black women upon the aforementioned cabinet posts. Therefore, subsequent to the second election of Barack Obama to the U.S. Presidency, semi-structured, one-on-one interviews were conducted with professional black women of varying ages, educational levels, disciplines, occupations, and work sectors to further probe the sentiments relayed during the above referenced conversations. Likewise, the interviews were conducted to explore professional black women's perceptions of the media and its portrayal of black women, and professional black women particularly. (See Table 5.1 for sample demographics.)

Overall Stereotypes

When asked to detail the stereotypes that they believe are often associated with black women, on a consistent basis, all of the participants replied with the same stereotypes historically and presently associated with black women including but not limited to "angry," "incompetent," "loud," "unintelligent," and "easily agitated." Because of these stereotypes, several participants stated that they make a concerted effort to go out of their way in order to dispel the prevailing perceptions of black women. One participant, the human resources

Table 5.1   Demographics of Semi-Structured Interview Respondents

Occupation/Title	Sector	Highest Educational Attainment	Identified Age Range	Time in Profession
Administrative Assistant	Legal	Bachelor's	30–35	10 years
Administrative Associate	Higher Education	Master's	50–55	9 years
Associate Director	Non-Profit	Doctorate	55–60	5 years
College Professor at 2-Year Institution	Higher Education	Master's	40–45	7 years
College Professor at 4-Year Institution	Higher Education	Doctorate	50–55	5 years
Human Resources Specialist	International Non-Government Organization	Master's	40–45	17 years
Lobbyist	Non-Profit	Doctorate	40–45	10 years
Program Assistant	Federal Government	High School Diploma	55–60	15 years
Provost	Higher Education	Doctorate	50–55	2 years
Teacher	Primary Education	Bachelor's	20–25	3 months

specialist, commented, "I've noticed that (non-black) people's approach to me is very careful. (However), once they get to know me and my capabilities there's more interaction." The above comment reflected that of other participants who stated that they feel as if they have to prove their capabilities in order to work effectively with their peers. Even once they have demonstrated their capabilities, participants indicated that the responses of their peers are often insulting and wounding. For instance, as the lobbyist explained, whenever she makes a relevant observation or statement in the presence of her peers, she overhears, "I always forget how smart she is." Similarly, another participant, the provost, remarked that, whenever we do something that shows our capability, "there's a response of surprise."

Professional Contributions Overlooked

Participants stated that there is a perception that they are supposed to do their job—and then some. The following responses and comments reflect the findings of a previous public health study that explored the impact of the "strong black woman" trope on the overall lived experiences of black women (Peacock and Black 2011). As one participant, the associate director of a non-profit, described, "We're perceived as strong and invincible. That works against us. They throw everything but the kitchen sink at us [to burden]." Yet, participants explained that when they do more than what is expected, their contributions are often overlooked or minimized. As the associate director further expressed, "They see us as strong, but they try to weaken us." Echoing her assertions, two participants in the higher education sector explicitly used the term "AcadeMammy," a term used to highlight the stereotype of the mammy still covertly imposed on black women within the modern day academic setting to describe their respective experiences in working with their peers and superiors. One of the participants, a community college professor, explained,

> Everybody thinks we're the AcadeMammy. White males want us to take care of them and help them do their jobs. Blacks too. [But] they don't want to pay us for the extra work we do. My former dean would put extra students in my class . . . Over the class limit! Because he knew I could handle it . . . However, he didn't want to pay me for taking on the extra students . . . because they don't want to reward or recognize us but they want us to carry the burden. It's as if they say, "You're capable. You can do it." At the same time, they don't want to perceive us as competent.

In the same manner, the university professor made the same observation. She too noted that the efforts, contributions, and accomplishments of black women are often taken for granted. Additionally, the participant observed that this is especially the case in those fields that are predominantly occupied by women such as education. The participant continued to note, that because black women are often taken for granted and expected to do more than their male counterparts without support or the necessary resources, it is also her perception that she is expected to fulfill the role of the "AcadeMammy." The participant imparted that it is her perception that, if she does not conform to the role and the expectations associated with the role, then she is ostracized for rejecting or challenging the prevailing stereotypes and that which is the norm for, or comfortable to, others.

The Media and Professional Black Women

Participants consistently identified the media as a source of the stereotypes that they must challenge on a daily basis within their respective work spaces. Initially, when discussing black women within the media, interview participants consistently stated that, in general, black women are scant. The lobbyist, for instance, briefly criticized, "In mainstream [media], you see the same five black female celebrities like Beyonce, Gabrielle Union, Kerry Washington, etc." Thus, when probed explicitly about professional black women in the media, participants overwhelmingly and emphatically exclaimed that, aside from those shown in black media outlets, there are too few, if any. As the program assistant acknowledged, "Black Enterprise does a good job of showing black female role models, but aside from that . . . (her voice trailed off)"

Continuing in that fashion, another participant remarked, "you see a lot of white women [portrayed in professional occupations] . . . For black women, when you do see us, either you see [us shown as] an inarticulate secretary or uptight, angry, and mean."

Of those professional black female characters seen in the media, participants expounded that, although they are portrayed in professional occupations, they are often shown in a negative light. As the non-profit associate director remarked, "Again, they're [shown as] unusually strong and [capable of] anything." Comparably, the university professor quipped, "There's Olivia Pope [on *Scandal*] and Mary Jane [on *Being Mary Jane*] [but] they're penalized for their work, or their personal lives are critiqued. People are more concerned with who they're sleeping with." The same participant also explained that she could only identify one professional black woman portrayed in a positive light. Even so, adding to that revelation, the participant observed that the one black woman pictured positively was rarely seen actively engaged in her professional work space. As she further revealed, "There was Claire Huxtable, but you never got to see her at work [in her profession]. [As a consequence], you don't get to see [any representation of] the impact that [professional black women] are making in their communities."

Several of the participants commented that the lack of black women seen in professional roles can largely be attributed to the roles, such as that of mammy or sapphire, in which black women have historically been portrayed. Therefore, when a black woman is depicted in a role outside of that which is stereotypical, many find it hard to accept. For example, one of the participants noted that, when the Oscar-nominated actress, Viola Davis, debuted on the popular television show, *How To Get Away With Murder,* as a highly successful attorney and law professor, the popular, mainstream magazine *People* posted on social media a racially offensive message that clearly illustrated their perception of her as the stereotypical mammy. To be explicit, the message, a less than overt signal to her role as the inarticulate housekeeper in the film, *The Help* read, "Waiting for Viola to break into 'You is kind. You is smart. You is impo'tant'" (Gupta 2014). Accordingly, other participants also affirmed that the mammy stereotype has been so ingrained into the collective consciousness of the general citizenry, that it overshadows images of black women depicted in professional occupations.

Black Women In and Out of the Political Arena—Same Story

Participants were questioned as to whether, and to what degree, there existed any parallels between the depictions of professional black women in general and the depictions of black female politicians. Once more, participants consistently replied that black female politicians are seldom, if ever, highlighted within the media. On the contrary, participants repeatedly responded that white female politicians are often seen in the media. As an example, the lobbyist recounted a publication recently released entitled, "Moms on the Hill." The publication featured female legislators and their families. According to the lobbyist, "Everyone in there was white." The lack of black females shown with their families or partners was a salient issue for a few of the participants, as they contended that failing to show black women with their families makes them appear ungrounded. Furthermore, participants noted that, because black female politicians are rarely shown with their families, it facilitates a "gender bending" process that makes black women politicians appear as masculine, and thus, aggressive. Thus, unlike the survey participants highlighted in Chapter 4 who commented that women are unfairly expected to be with their families, interview participants noted that, when *black* women are not seen with their families, it has an adverse impact on their image.

In addition, several of the participants followed up their statements on the lack of black female politicians seen in the media with statements contending that, on the rare occasions when black female politicians are seen in the media, it is usually within an overly negative light. While the program assistant contended, "(the media) slanders black female politicians," the teacher made a similar assertion saying, "white female politicians don't seem to be questioned or viewed as negatively as black female politicians." The lobbyist provided an in-depth description of black female politicians' representation in the media.

> Black female politicians do not get a lot of [attention] in the media. When the media does focus on them, they tend to portray them as being aggressive . . . And having masculine characteristics . . . They often show them as angry. However, I think people are confusing passion with anger and [fostering] perceptions of a lack of femininity [on the part of black female politicians].

Such depictions, according to the university professor, impacts black female politicians' ability to effectively create or influence public policy. Because black women politicians are seen as angry rather than compassionate, they, unlike white men who are frequently shown as fervent about issues relevant to them, must be overly nice. Along the same vein, referencing the impact of the media's depiction of black female professionals in and out of the political sphere, the community college professor explained, "Black female politicians [I sense] feel constrained. [Black women professionals] want to work for our communities, but you have to work within a power structure." Hence, according to participants, because of the power structure upheld by media stereotypes, many professional black women in or outside of the political sphere must contend with the same issues pertaining to capability versus prevailing stereotypes. As the provost succinctly summed up, "Our experiences are very much the same. If we all got in the same room together, we may have different careers, but the story is still the same."

CONCLUSION

One can contend that the historical underrepresentation of women, and women of color particularly, within the national political arena was initially born out of the explicitly inscribed characterization of the U.S. Presidency as seen through the lenses of the authors of the United States Constitution, and in due course, the architects of the U.S. government. As the document remains the reigning blue print for the political and legal operations of this country, it significantly impacted the degree to which women and/or racial minorities were included within the nation's democratic processes. Although it has, from time to time, been amended to reflect the increasing acceptance of historically marginalized persons, the original language specific to women and/or racial minorities serve as a reminder of the exclusive nature the United States Presidency has maintained until recently. Be that as it may, although the U.S. elected the first president of color, the national political arena continues to be largely white and/or male. To further this point, voters recently elected a record number of women to the U.S. Congress. Even still, both branches of the U.S. government, continue to be largely dominated by and/or associated with white males. Therefore, it may also be concluded that biases persist regarding elected political positions on a national scale.

As outlined and revealed, the primary source of gender and/or racial biases stem from the media depictions of women and/or black women in particular. Media outlets persist in reifying traditional gender notions that undermine the perception of women as leaders. Unfortunately, when introducing race into the equation, media depictions often rely on and maintain the long-standing stereotypes associated with black women resulting in a cyclical pattern that distorts the collective perception of black women. For this reason, black female politicians have and continue to endure disparaging depictions that potentially discourage voter support. It may be asserted as well that the well-publicized traumatic experiences of select black female politicians at the hands of the media may also discourage other black females from entering the national political arena.

Interviews conducted with professional black women revealed that, it too, was their perception that the media has proven to be a fundamental cause of the interpersonal challenges they encounter within the workplace. Overall, the vast majority of those interviewed explained that the depictions of black women in the media has greatly influenced the manner in which their counterparts and co-workers interact with them, often requiring many of them to prove themselves unlike the prevailing stereotypes in order to be respected as competent and skilled specialists within their respective fields. Interview respondents consistently remarked that the depictions of black women within the media has also adversely impacted black women within the national political arena. Participants likewise observed that the virtual absence of black female politicians, with the exception of controversial and less than positive, well-rounded depictions of black female politicians propagates stereotypes of them placing them at a continued disadvantage.

Chapter 6

Networks and Campaign Funding

Past studies have probed the role of networks, traditionally defined as a linkage of social and professional relationships, in spurring political participation (Sokhey and Djupe 2011; Lim 2008). Those studies have, however, looked at the manner in which social relationships have influenced whether or not one engages in voting, electioneering, campaigning, and so on. Such activities are vital in any election, but they are not the sole activities or efforts that are important to a successful campaign. One could even contend that such activities or efforts would not be possible without one of the single most important components of a successful campaign—funding. Without a doubt, fundraising is one of the first efforts that a candidate must consider prior to moving forward with a political campaign.

In today's political climate, significant fundraising activities, via exploration committees, for instance, may take place before a candidate officially announces their intent to pursue an elected office (Sebold, Limbocker, Dowdle, and Stewart 2011). And almost invariably, upon the announcement, media outlets begin to investigate and report the amount of funding raised by the newly recognized candidate (Hamburger and Gold 2015; Miller 2014). A candidate in possession of healthy campaign coffers usually suggests to other potential donors or supporters that the candidate has the necessary resources to pursue a campaign, and more importantly, a successful one (Merica 2015). Significant fundraising is certainly an essential when launching a campaign for a state or national office. In recent election cycles, presidential campaigns have evolved into non-stop fundraising operations in order to allow for the implementation of a comprehensive strategy aimed at gaining voter support. According to Adkins and Dowdle, for national campaigns, early campaign financing allows presidential candidates not only to establish multiple state offices simultaneously, it also allows presidential candidates to contract the services of political consultants, advisors, and staff to guide and manage the day-to-day operations of a political campaign (2002). The ability to secure and establish such workspace, resources, and staff is especially vital to the successful management of a national campaign in the present day political climate. Past presidential elections have demonstrated that early campaign financing, and specifically those financial resources garnered prior to primary season, has substantive and determining influence on whether or not a candidate secures a party's nomination (Adkins and Dowdle 2002).

Therefore, networks are essential to fundraising as well. Social and professional networks serve as pathways to accessing the necessary pecuniary sway that candidates require in a successful campaign bid. To be explicit, having access to the right people or organizations allows one to garner or generate the funds needed to operate an effective campaign (Witt, Paget, and Matthews 1995). Moreover, social networks also allow access to invaluable social capital that may translate or manifest into financial support. To be specific once more, social and professional networks function by connecting people with those who have authority or influence over others. In the context of politics, connecting candidates with key political players or leaders may result in financial support from professional and personal acquaintances of those leaders (Institute for Women's Policy Research 2015; Witt, Paget, and Matthews 1995). Such connections are also crucial to gaining endorsements that may result in additional support of varying kinds including individual monetary and volunteer assistance.

CAMPAIGN FUNDING AND GENDER

Just as women are often hesitant to run for office due to stereotypes surrounding the relationship between gender and innate leadership abilities, empirical evidence also reveals that women are more hesitant to run for elected office due to perceived challenges associated with fundraising (Ford 2011). Tapping into networks for the purposes of financing the campaigns of women candidates has historically been challenging. As political scholars have discussed in their respective analyses of women donor networks, men were once the sole manager of the household checkbook (Ford 2011; Witt, Paget, and Matthews 1995). Therefore, women were once restricted in their capacity to support other women seeking political office. Similarly, because of gender disparities in access to capital or assets grounded in the historically systemic restriction of women from business enterprises, they have encountered tremendous stress, and/or difficulty, in financing their own campaigns or generating the seed money vital to attracting supplemental donors needed to sustain a long-term campaign (Strauss 2002).

Although men candidates have expressed their lack of enthusiasm for fundraising, women candidates especially detest fundraising in part due to their perceptions that male candidates experience less fundraising challenges since male candidates have been known to rely on large sums of money from fewer, individual donors known to them through their respective personal and professional relationships, or plainly stated, their social networks (Ford 2011; Crespin 2010; Jenkins 2007). To compensate, and remain competitive, women candidates are more likely to tap into more heterogeneous sources or methods of campaign financing to circumvent the reliance on a smaller, select donor pool (Jenkins 2007). The utilization of smaller amounts of monies from larger groups or numbers of people to fund campaign efforts is however an often daunting and tiresome task for many women candidates (Ford 2011).

WOMEN AND POLITICAL ACTION COMMITTEES

Although women have experienced collective advancements in the professional workforce, and thus income, fundraising, even in the present day, continues to be a trial for women seeking elected office (Institute for Women's Policy Research 2015). Like their male counterparts, women candidates have become increasingly reliant on the support provided by political action committees. Political action committees first emerged in 1944 when the Congress of Industrial Organizations (CIO) was founded to raise money to aid in the re-election of Franklin Delano Roosevelt (Sabato 1985). Since then, countless other political action committees, more commonly known simply as PACs, have continued to provide support to those candidates whose platforms coincide with their respective interests (Sabato 1985).

Among the many PACs currently existing within the United States, several have the explicit goal of providing support to women candidates. Since their emergence, female candidates have become more competitive in raising funds relative to their male counterparts (Ford 2011). Although a couple of earlier established women's PACS such as The Women's Campaign Fund (1974) and The National Women's Political Caucus (1971) were created with the goal of supporting women regardless of their respective political party affiliation, others that are openly partisan have since emerged (e.g., the Republican Party's Women in the Senate and House [WISH List]) (Witt, Paget, and Matthews 1995). The most prominent example is EMILY's List, the brainchild of Ellen Malcolm who, in 1985, identified women candidates' need for campaign seed money (Ford 2011; Smooth 2006; Witt, Paget, and Matthews 1995). The PAC's name, in fact, is an acronym for Early Money Is Like Yeast—an acknowledgment of the imperative nature of seed money in the contemporary political fundraising climate (Ford 2011; Witt, Paget, and

Matthews 1995). EMILY's List works by maintaining an enormous national network of donors who agree to pay a membership fee. On top of the membership fee, members also agree to pay an additional fee in support of those candidates selected by EMILY's List. In addition to funding, EMILY's List also provides strategic campaign support including mailings and ground support (Burrell 2006). An endorsement from EMILY's List has proven to galvanize support from other constituency groups (Smooth 2006). Each female Democrat elected to the U.S. House of Representatives for the first time in 2004 had the endorsement of EMILY's List (Burrell 2006).

Receiving seed money and other support from EMILY's List is not simply a matter of picking up the phone and asking for a donation. In order to receive the monetary and strategic support from EMILY's List, several criteria must first be met. First and foremost, candidates requesting support from EMILY's list must be both pro-choice and Democratic at a minimum. Securing early seed money from EMILYs List mandates potential candidates demonstrate or provide evidence of their candidates sustainability via polls, and if there is an incumbent, the likelihood of defeating the incumbent (i.e., What are the incumbent's weak areas? Where are they exposed?) (Witt, Paget, and Matthews 1995). Still, as mentioned, the popular PAC requires potential seed money recipients provide polls as evidence of viability, which are expensive to conduct. Thus, candidates must be able to access or generate funds in order to simply secure additional early funding, another demonstrative example of the role of networks with access to capital in the current political climate. EMILY's List nonetheless has become an effective mainstay in the political arena opening doors of access to women candidates (Burrell 2006; Smooth 2006). In 2014, EMILY's List boasted a donor network of three million. Moreover, during the 2014 election cycle alone, it raised over $25 million to aid in the launch and maintenance of multiple Congressional campaigns, further solidifying its role in the realm of campaign financing (Chang 2014).

Exemplary Reflections: Black Women and Campaign Funding in the Past

Although women in general have made strides in fundraising, women of color, and African-American woman especially, are likely to face uphill battles in fundraising within such an environment. Historical examples provide a glimpse into the challenges faced by women of color within the state and national political fundraising arenas. Two of the more well-known instances illustrate the unique challenges faced by political candidates standing at the nexus of race and gender.

Former U.S. House Representative Shirley Chisolm, being the first example, made history more than once during her lifetime. She initially made history in 1968 when she was elected to represent New York's 12th Congressional District, one of many majority-minority districts created as a result of the Voting Rights Act of 1965 (Chisolm 2010). As the only woman in her Congressional freshmen class, Congresswoman Chisolm often challenged the status quo long existing within the government establishment (Sinclair-Chapman and Price 2008). Despite resistance from the establishment, but in an effort to further represent the issues of minorities and low-income persons residing in urban areas, Congresswoman Chisolm announced her bid for the U.S. Presidency in 1972 (Chisolm 2010; Sinclair-Chapman and Price 2008). In announcing her intentions to pursue the U.S. Presidency, she became the first African-American major party candidate *and* the first woman to seek the nomination of the national Democratic Party. Although her intent was to continue to bring to light those issues most often faced by marginalized communities, Representative Chisolm ironically faced opposition from her African-American male peers within the House. True to the even greater patriarchal nature of the national political arena at that time, Representative Chisolm's male colleagues within the Congressional Black Caucus (CBC) contended that she had not consulted with them prior to initiating her bid for the U.S. Presidency (Chisolm 2010; Sinclair-Chapman and Price 2008). Aside from her colleagues in the CBC, well-known leaders of the National Organization for Women (NOW), an organization that she helped to found, did not endorse her (Smooth 2014). In the end, the lack of support from members of her own party resulted in a severe lack of the funding necessary to sustain a national campaign. Due to the lack of funding, and subsequently the capacity and resources to galvanize voter support, Representative Chisolm's bid for the U.S. Presidency failed to progress beyond the Democratic National Convention where she received 10 percent of the total delegate vote (Chisolm 2010).

In a more recent example, following in the footsteps of Representative Chisolm, and after a successful political career on the state level, Carol Moseley-Braun entered the national political arena in 1992. The year 1992 is frequently dubbed the "Year of the Woman" due to the record number of women who were elected to the U.S. Congress that year with the Anita Hill testimonies playing no small part in the galvanization of the female electorate (Rudin 2003). (It should be noted that, while the number of women elected to the U.S. Senate that year was considered a record, the total number of new women entering the U.S. Senate was four, or .04 percent of the total U.S. Senate body in proportional terms, an egregious under representation of the U.S. female population.) In addition to being the first and only since African-American woman to be elected to the U.S. Senate, she was only the second African-American to be elected to the U.S. Senate post-Reconstruction (Congressional Office of History n.d.). For many, she was simply viewed as a symbol of potentially growing diversity within the U.S. Senate—a notion that she rejected commenting that she was elected to be more than a symbol (National Public Radio 2003). Like Representative Chisolm, Senator Braun championed issues pertinent to women and persons of color. Of course, like Chisolm, Braun also experienced her fair share of intersecting racism and sexism from members of the political media (Smooth 2014). Unsurprisingly, regardless of her Congressional efforts and accomplishments on behalf of traditionally marginalized communities, former Senator Braun faced an uphill battle in a bid for re-election. During her one term as U.S. Senator, Braun contended with allegations of campaign fraud and financial mismanagement leading to a five-year-long investigation by the Federal Election Commission that determined an inconsistency totaling a mere $311 (National Public Radio 2003). However, the damage had been done (Tam 2014). Senator Braun was significantly overwhelmed in terms of campaign fundraising by her opponent who spent $12 million of his own money to secure Braun's former senate seat. One could contend that the allegations launched against former Senator Braun had reverberating effects (Tam 2014). Since her attempt at re-election to the U.S. Senate, former Senator Braun has launched two unsuccessful U.S. Presidential campaigns. Her campaign coffers were relatively empty in comparison to her competitors—who all happened to be male (Smooth 2014). Thus, the simple allegation or hint of campaign financing violations seemingly left an indelible mark on potential donors' willingness to support her in another national campaign.

Present Day: Black Women and Campaign Financing

Former Senator Braun's experience is particularly intriguing considering the comparative ease at which Secretary Hillary Clinton has raised money for her two U.S. Presidential bids. (She was significantly outspent during her first bid by now President Obama who relied heavily on digital donations, requiring her to use some of her personal funds, but nonetheless had access to a sizable amount of money.) One may recall that she and her husband, former U.S. President William J. Clinton, were implicated in the well-publicized Savings and Loan Scandal that had massive reverberations throughout the banking industry (Maraniss and Schmidt 1996). Regardless of what appeared to be plausible involvement on their part, through her network, she has been able to raise millions of dollars for a second time in preparation for the 2016 primary and, heavily anticipated, general elections. Hence, relative to Moseley-Braun, Clinton has had a considerably better experience in rebounding from public scandal and subsequently raising and accessing funds, suggesting, if only slightly, that although women in general contend with gender stereotypes, women of color face additional obstacles, especially in regard to fundraising.

Keeping that in mind, one must consider the impact of allegations of financial mismanagement on donors' and voters' support of black women politicians in general. Such allegations may serve to undermine the credibility of black women seeking the confidence of voter support who quite likely have been exposed to negative stereotypical depictions of women of color. As discussed in Chapter 5, U.S. Representative Maxine Waters had to contend with allegations of financial mismanagement and Congressional ethics violations (Helderman 2012). The allegations were covered with great scrutiny by media outlets, once more, reifying the notions of black women as untrustworthy and unprofessional (Bresnahan 2012; Helderman 2012; Harris-Perry 2011; Abrams 2011; Simon 2010). Although the charges were eventually dropped, the allegations alone will undoubtedly overshadow Representative Waters for the remainder of her political career.

It is the cumulative effects of such mere allegations against black female politicians that potentially have an enormous effect on the campaign fundraising outcomes of politicians who are both black and of the female gender. Utilizing data collected by the Center for Responsive Politics, a report written and released by the Center for American Women and Politics at Rutgers University in 2014 revealed that, in comparison to their male counterparts, black women within the U.S. House raised lower amounts of campaign funds. According to the report, this was true for open seat and incumbent Congressional House winners. Although there was only one black woman who won an open seat U.S. Congressional election in 2012, she raised $812,493 which was substantially less than the black men who won open seat U.S. Congressional elections upon raising an average of $1,448,192. In examining funds raised by incumbent office holders within the CBC exclusively, male incumbent office holders raised over $150,000 more on average in comparison to their female counterparts. That is not to say that allegations of campaign fraud have unequivocally had a direct, negative impact on black female politicians' ability to raise campaign funds. However, such allegations definitely do not help.

STRUCTURAL BARRIERS

As previously discussed, PACs have had an indisputable impact on electoral politics in the United States. Their support has enabled many, including those who were considered long shots, to declare victory (Burrell 2006; Smooth 2006). Recent changes to the manner in which they operate have had a costly ripple effect that is hard to ignore. Unless legislation or policies are put in place to stymie the impact of recent changes, such effects will undoubtedly continue to determine and shape campaign fundraising. More importantly, for those politicians, women politicians of color especially, who faced fundraising challenges prior to such changes, may view the recent changes as an additional barrier. Overcoming those challenges will require them to broaden their donor base.

Citizens United v. Federal Exchange Commission

EMILY's List is one of the many PACs with influence on the campaign financing and overall election process. In accordance with their general purpose, PACs have facilitated the generation of large sums of money to support candidates, or candidates' issues, that reflect their respective ideological or political leanings (Ford 2011; Smooth 2006; Sabato 1985). Thus, due to the amount of funding required to launch and maintain a national campaign, PACs in general have become perfunctory components of the fundraising activities associated with the electoral process. Their presence has undoubtedly enabled countless political candidates to get elected. Yet, despite their foothold in the political arena, they have, until recently, functioned under some semblance of governmental regulation to provide a seemingly neutral playing field for those seeking elected office. In short, to prevent those with unlimited financial resources from monopolizing the political playing field, federal law required that PACs abide by very precise rules. One such rule, for example, being the amount of money an individual could donate to a PAC.

This all came to an end in 2010 when the U.S. Supreme Court decided in the case of *Citizens United v. the Federal Election Commission* that campaign donations are a form of free speech, and placing limits on freedom of speech was a violation of a corporation's right to speak on a political subject. Due to the Court's decision, PACs as they were once known underwent what was an almost immediate transformation. One could, and with very little difficulty, contend that corporations, multimillionaires, billionaires, and business executives were essentially given carte blanche over campaign financing, and in turn, the political process. The elimination of restrictions on the amount an individual or corporation can donate has already had enormous repercussions and results. Under the previous laws that governed PACs and campaign financing, direct candidate advocacy and electioneering were not permissible by PACs. PACs could solicit funding for the strict purposes of issue advocacy, more than likely an issue known to be supported by the candidate of their choice. Also, under previous PAC regulations, electioneering within 60 days of an election was prohibited. Now, because of the 2010 *Citizens United* ruling, outside spending groups are permitted to voice their explicit and direct support for the candidate of their choice via media advertising. And they may do it within 60 days of an election.

Because of the Court's decision, many have contended that PACs have been replaced by super PACs—outside spending groups with the ability to solicit and accept limitless funding in the form of individual and corporate contributions donations. More importantly, PACs with the ability to spend what can only be termed as insane amounts of money to sway an election in their favor. Spending figures since the Supreme Court decision speak for themselves. At one time, spending hundreds of millions of dollars to help get a national candidate elected was seen as astronomical. Currently, or post-*Citizens United*, spending hundreds of millions on advertising alone has become the "new norm." During the last U.S. presidential election, the two candidates combined each spent several hundred million dollars on campaign operations. The amount of dollars spent on starting and maintaining a national campaign is only expected to increase due to the effects of *Citizens United*. Funding totals revealed by the Center for Responsive Politics shows a hard to ignore trend in the increasingly intimate relationship between money and politics.

In 2010, the year of the *Citizens United* Supreme Court decision, conservative super PACs spent $36.7 million as liberal super PACs spent $24.6 million (Center for Responsive Politics n.d.). Relatively speaking, such numbers are actually rather small. In truth, the limited amounts spent during 2010 may be attributed to the fact there was no presidential election that year. However, not to be overlooked, 2010 was the last Congressional mid-term election that resulted in a noticeable shift in power within the U.S. House of Representatives as Republicans became the majority party. Thus, the amount of money spent by outside conservative groups had the intended effect. The same intended effect did not occur in 2012. Just two years after the *Citizens United* decision, the year of the last U.S. presidential election, an exponential explosion in funding occurred with conservative super PACs spending $406.8 million and liberal super PACs spending $195.5 million in support of their respective candidates—again, a mere two years after *Citizens United* (Center for Responsive Politics n.d.). (Although super PACs also supported congressional candidates that particular year, the majority of funds were directed to presidential candidates. Despite their efforts, President Obama was re-elected to the U.S. Presidency.)

Compounding matters are the number of "dark money" groups forming as a result of *Citizens United*. "Dark money" groups are non-profits that are not required to publicly report their individual or corporate donors, but they are permitted to spend funds against or in support of political campaigns in the same manner as for-profit organizations. The result—over $300 million, combined from conservative and liberal "dark money" groups, spent on political campaigns in 2012 with $140,199,676 spent on the U.S. Presidential race (Center for Responsive Politics n.d.). This is a huge increase from the combined $5 million given by conservative and liberal non-profit groups in 2006.

With the ability to donate unprecedented amounts of money with little to no accountability, wealthy donors and magnanimous organizations now have the power to virtually mold national politics and the competing candidates to fit their policy needs.

The Current Socioeconomic Status of Minority Networks

Although it has been documented and acknowledged that women are less willing to ask for campaign donations outright, black women seeking elected offices within federal (and state) legislative bodies may face a unique hurdle unrelated to the *willingness* to solicit campaign funds. As noted earlier, black women began entering the federal legislative bodies upon the creation of black majority districts as a result of the Voting Rights Act of 1965 (Smooth 2006). Similarly, in 1992, twelve more black women entered the federal legislative body with the formation of 12 additional majority-minority districts in the southern part of the United States (Center for American Women and Politics 2015). Consequently, for the most part, African-American women's mobility into national politics has been as a result of concentrated numbers of minorities within a voting district. Such districts often have within them disproportionate numbers of low-income persons due to the historically inextricable link between race and socioeconomic status born out of discriminatory practices such as redlining and predatory mortgage lending (Morris 2009; Dedman 2001; Schemo 2001; Conley 2001). Adding to that, the disparate accumulation of wealth between whites and their racial and ethnic counterparts, who are most likely to support women politicians of color, may in large part be attributed to the inability to inherit property and other forms of capital due to long-standing policies and practices born out of slavery and other forms of de jure and de facto discrimination (DuBois 1935).

On a more positive note however, one would be remiss to overlook the changing educational levels, and consequently socioeconomic status, of racial and ethnic minorities. According to a 2014 report by the National Center for Education Statistics, between 1990 and 2013, the percentage of blacks and Hispanics 25–29 years old who held a high school diploma or its equivalent increased from 82 to 90 percent and 58 to 76 percent respectively (U.S. Department of Education 2014) Similarly, although the postsecondary gap between whites and racial and ethnic minorities actually widened during the same period due to simultaneous increases among whites, the percentage of blacks with a bachelor's degree increased from 13 to 20 percent and eight to 16 percent for Hispanics nonetheless (U.S. Department of Education 2014). Once more, the increases in education among racial and ethnic minorities is unambiguously a contributing factor to economic and social improvements among racial and ethnic minorities overall. Although persons of color remain disproportionately prevalent among the working and low-income classes, many have gradually joined the ranks of the middle-class with a notable proportion even entering the ranks of the upper echelon enjoying enormous amounts of wealth. Thus, even though racial and ethnic minorities continue to lag behind whites in terms of educational attainment and corresponding income and wealth, they are, however, obtaining higher levels of education than in the past.

Yet again, adding an additional layer of complexity, in comparison to their white middle-class counterparts, upper-middle and middle-class racial and ethnic minorities continue to earn lower incomes and accumulate lower amounts of wealth, placing them at a disadvantage in terms of providing significant or discernable financial backing to political candidates. Succinctly acknowledged above, persons of color continue to face challenges in obtaining socioeconomic parity with their white counterparts. Chief among those reasons remains systemic discrimination in a range of forms. As a representative example, a study conducted by Gaddis in 2014 illustrated blacks or African-Americans in possession of postsecondary degrees from elite universities are still less likely to secure employment in comparison to their white peers. In a similar fashion, African-American and Hispanic women with postsecondary and postgraduate degrees consistently earn less than their white male counterparts (Bureau of Labor Statistics 2016; American Association of University Women 2014). As a result, despite attaining postsecondary degrees, discriminatory actions throughout the labor market prevent qualified persons of color from earning incomes that would propel them to the upper and/or upper-middle classes and provide them with the financial and accompanying social capital to fundamentally impact national political representation.

The Rich. The Powerful.

As a consequence, African-American women seeking elected office may be more reliant upon social networks that lack the comparable capital and financial resources of those networks that are making significant contributions to national campaigns. For instance, an October 2015 investigative piece by the *New York Times* shared that only 158 families have provided more than half of the financial support for early campaigns efforts leading up to the 2016 U.S. presidential election. Of the 158 families, the lion's share, 138 to be exact, are white, male, and conservative or right-leaning. Only 20 of the individuals or their corporations are supporting left-leaning or candidates within the Democratic Party, the party to which many, or even most, registered voters and politicians of color respectively belong and support.

Such a demographic distribution reveals a pattern that is likely to continue given the board composition of Fortune 500 companies. A 2002 article by

USA Today revealed that, in the twenty-first century, a dearth of women and people of color remained on corporate boards (Strauss). Moreover, the article illustrated that, in accordance with C. Wright Mills' Power Elite Theory, a concentration of a relatively small number of people held appointments on multiple boards, solidifying the non-penetrable shield of exclusivity around the exclusive network within corporate America (Kentor and Jang 2004; Farganis 2000; Berberoglu 1998). Slightly more than a decade later, an analysis conducted by Domhoff, who has consistently argued that an elite group of rich and powerful individuals work to influence the actions of policy analysts and creators, showed that the large number of white males on corporate boards persists (Berberoglu 1998). He further noted that the number of white males on corporate boards is actually an overrepresentation of the white male population in the United States. Conversely, he discovered that although the number of white women on corporate boards has increased in recent years, the number of persons of color have simultaneously decreased (Domhoff, 2013). As a result, the number of persons of color on corporate boards is disproportionately lower relative to the total number of persons of color in the United States. For those who are both women *and* persons of color on corporate boards, the proportion was below two percent (Domhoff 2013). Therefore, men and women candidates of color may continue to experience fewer opportunities to form relationships or networks with those whose lived experiences, and therefore political ideology, is likely to be similar or conducive to their own. This particularly daunting in the current money-driven political climate. This is especially crucial again considering Philpot and Walton observed black women are more likely to support black women candidates (2007).

This is not to say that white males are not willing to support a woman of color in pursuit of a national office. However, as noted in an article by David Eldon, the vast majority of those occupying seats on corporate boards are not only white and male, they are older and have primarily interacted solely with those who are reflective of their images—aesthetically and ideologically (2013). Therefore, they are likely to find comfort in their continued support of those political candidates with whom they can identify on both counts.

One of the most widely referenced historical examples of the relationship between wealth and politics is that of the Kennedy family. The Kennedy name has become synonymous with the wealth, power, privilege, and exclusivity that often accompanies national politics. The genesis of the Kennedys' stronghold on national politics began with Joseph Kennedy, Sr., a Harvard-educated bank executive who made a fortune as a stock trader. He was later appointed as chairman of the United States Securities and Exchange Commission (SEC), and thereafter, the United States Ambassador to Britain. His foray into politics came as a result of his support of Franklin

D. Roosevelt, who in turn appointed the Kennedy, Sr. to his position at the SEC (Dallek 2004). After losing one of his four sons in World War II, the Kennedy patriarch made a conscious decision to prime his surviving three sons for careers in politics. Using his wealth and connections, the patriarch enabled and encouraged his sons, each Harvard-educated, to pursue successful political endeavors (Dallek 2004). All three served as U.S. Senators at some point in their respective careers and one son, Robert Kennedy, served as U.S. Attorney General under another son, John F. Kennedy, who served as the 35th U.S President. Combined the three Kennedy brothers served almost 70 years in national offices further establishing the Kennedys' place within the political hierarchy and allowing younger Kennedy generations to enter into the national political arena.

Another well-known personification of the relationship between wealth and politics would, without a doubt, be the Koch brothers. Like the Kennedys, the Koch brothers received top notch educations with three of the four attending their father's alma mater, the Massachusetts Institute of Technology, where he also held a seat on the board (Mayer 2016). Of the four sons born to Fred Koch, a scientist and entrepreneur who was an unyielding advocate of small government and least restrictive economic policies, Charles and David are the two most politically involved. Charles and David, estimated to have a net worth of $40 billion each, have continued in their father's footsteps. In doing so, they have earned themselves a reputation as being supportive, and especially generous, to start-up organizations, think tanks, and theorists which strive to advance conservative social and economic policies (Mayer 2016; Benac 2015). This reputation was not earned haphazardly. Beginning in the latter part of the twentieth century, as part of their plan to create a pervasive conservative network, the Koch brothers, along with other corporate executives that shared the same political and economic ideologies, started to sponsor the professional pursuits of like-minded economic scholars and theorists in an attempt to influence public policy (Mayer 2016). Their efforts can be credited for sparking the modern conservative movement in politics. As Mayer noted in her book *Dark Money: The Hidden History of the Billionaires Behind the Rise of the Radical Right*, the intricate and capacious political network, or machine, devised by the Koch brothers came to be named the "Kochtopus" (2016).

In a more direct fashion, the Koch brothers have also made campaign donations in support of right-wing political candidates. For instance, during the last presidential campaign cycle, the Koch brothers donated a total of $400 million to support the GOP efforts to clinch the U.S. Presidency. Multiple outlets have reported that the Koch brothers plan to top that amount, as they have allocated close to $900 million to provide support to issue advocacy and political activities. Considering their dogged support of conservative efforts in the past, the $900 million will undoubtedly be directed to support political advocacy and activities that are reflective of their conservative record.

Both families are demonstrative examples of how enormous wealth can be utilized to foster intimate networks that have far reaching impacts. Although the Kennedy brothers were more left-leaning in their politics, they are a reflection of the exclusive nature inherent within national politics. Unlike the Kennedys, the Koch brothers were not actual politicians themselves but advocated, designed, and funded exclusive networks that promoted conservative social and economic policies.

OBAMA'S GAME CHANGER: DIGITAL DONATIONS

Leading up to his historical election in 2008, President Obama made other historic moves. Unlike countless presidential candidates who had come before him, President Obama chose to forego public financing. He chose instead to rely strictly on private donations to fund his campaign. While some may have viewed the decision as a risky, his decision proved to be extremely beneficial (and literally valuable) to his campaign. True to his grassroots beginnings, Obama relied on a grassroots approach to help fund his campaign (Luo 2008). Using the internet, Obama solicited donations from at $1 and up. People who were inspired by his campaign message and the historical importance of his candidacy regularly donated to his campaign (Vargas 2011). Ultimately, Obama boasted campaign coffers totaling approximately $500 million via digital donations (Okpalaoka 2012). His Republican challenger, John McCain, was outspent preventing him from having a ground support system comparable to that of the Obama campaign.

In 2011, President Obama raised an even greater amount of funds from digital donations. To be exact, President Obama raised over $600 million from donors who made contributions utilizing his campaign website (Okpalaoka 2012). Citing the results of a study, a *Washington Post* article assessed a sizable proportion of President Obama's donations came from small donations—defined as $200 or less (Eggen 2012). The total amount generated by small donations equaled to $56.7 million, greater than the total he raised in small donations during his previous presidential campaign (Eggen 2012). Although President Obama also raised funds utilizing the traditional approach of expensive or celebrity-laden dinners, he demonstrated during both campaign cycles that smaller donations, in aggregate form, can be impactful. Following President Obama's digital donation model, at the close of January 2016, the campaign managers of U.S. Presidential candidate Senator Bernie Sanders revealed a draw of $20 million for the month. The total amount was the result of small donations made online. Calculations determined that the average donor gave $27. Therefore, the use of the internet as a campaign fundraising tool is invaluable and increasingly necessary in the current technology dependent society.

CONCLUSION

Women have made strides in campaign financing. In comparison to the challenges once faced by women in the arena of campaign financing, collectively, women are now fundraising powerhouses. Political fundraising organizations such as EMILY's List have proven to be formidable in aiding women candidates seeking election to political office, including national offices. Nonetheless, recent changes to campaign financing laws may potentially prove to be significantly challenging. For veteran women politicians who have established donor networks, navigating the challenges presented by the new campaign laws may not be difficult. However, for those candidates who may be new to the political arena and/or experiencing trepidation about running for office, the recent changes may serve as a source of discouragement. Also of concern are women of color. Results shared by the Center of American Women and Politics revealed that women of color within the CBC raised noticeably fewer campaign dollars than their male counterparts, hinting that women of color seeking to launch political campaigns connected to the national political arena may have to operate with fewer resources in the present high-stakes era of campaign financing.

Adding to the potential conundrum, the most powerful networks remain the most exclusive networks. They also remain overwhelmingly white, male, and conservatively leaning. This naturally presents a potential hurdle to those candidates who are demographically and ideologically the diametric opposite. To ameliorate and navigate the potential obstacles or changes posed by *Citizens United*, women and women of color, particularly one seeking to occupy the Oval Office, should study and adopt the development and use of grassroots approaches in order to tap into an expansive network of supporters who are willing to give but unable to afford the admission of a big-ticket fundraiser (e.g., $1,000 a plate dinners).

Chapter 7

The Voting Rights Act

Twenty-First Century Changes and Application

Chapter 6 presented an analysis of the campaign funding challenges faced by many current and potential politicians, especially women and women of color particularly. And while funding is one of the greatest hurdles that candidates must overcome, garnering the necessary votes to ultimately win the sought after office is just as great a challenge. Granted, campaign funding is an imperative to attract voter support via strategic operations including, but not limited to, consistent and long-term media coverage and advertising. However, political candidates are not alone in overcoming hurdles within the American democratic process. Reflecting on America's civil rights past, the right to vote has not always been an automatic one for select persons among the American constituency, thereby making the right to vote one of the hardest earned civil rights possessed by individual citizens. Consequently, those who elect the candidates to represent them within the governing body have and, to an extent, continue to overcome hurdles as well.

The right to vote is an integral component of societal governance. It has been said many times and in various ways that voting is in its simplest form democracy in action. Voting allows citizens to elect those leaders that they believe will represent their respective social, political, and economic interests. It is no surprise then that the right to vote has often captured the time and attention of government officials and citizens. Historically, much effort and sacrifice has been made to expand the right to vote beyond the demographic to which it was once limited—white and male. As discussed in Chapter 4, the 15th Amendment to the United States Constitution, also known as one of the three Civil Rights Amendments, granted the right to vote to those slaves made free per the 13th Amendment. Years later, in 1920, the 19th Amendment was ratified thereby granting the right to vote to eligible female U.S. citizens as well. With the 15th and 19th Constitutional

Amendments removing racial and/or gender barriers from the voting process, the twentieth century brought a sense of hope for many who had previously been disenfranchised.

Many persons of color, African-Americans particularly, soon learned that, although the Constitution broadly granted the right to vote regardless of race and/or gender, it did not make provisions to prevent exclusionary actions and policies on the state and county level (Branch 1988). Actions and policies employed by county- and state-level officials, notably in the Deep South, included, but were not limited to, poll taxes, literacy tests, grandfather clauses, and other purposive administrative obstacles (Giddings 2006; Branch 1988). Non-official tactics employed, and arguably sanctioned or conveniently overlooked by county- and state-level officials, included physical and verbal harassment and intimidation of African-Americans who attempted to vote or whites who assisted African-Americans in their attempt to vote (Sullivan 1999; Branch 1988). As a result of the policies and non-official actions directed toward and against African-Americans, many became discouraged or fearful and opted to not even attempt to register. In response, African-Americans and supporters of African-American suffrage engaged in civil disobedience via nonviolent protests (Aguiar 1999; Sullivan 1999). Often times, their peaceful protests were met with arrests, attack dogs, and unmitigated police brutality. It was after the media's spotlight on the harassment and physical violence experienced by peaceful protestors seeking to exercise their Constitutional rights that the federal government acted. In as much, it was days after the march from Selma to Montgomery in March 1965 when news outlets spotlighted protestors that were mercilessly battered by police and civilian white supremacists, a day now known as "Bloody Sunday," that President Lyndon Johnson pushed for the passage of the Voting Rights Act of 1965 (Sullivan 1999).

In short, the Voting Rights Act of 1965 mandated that the federal government oversee all policies and actions of states and jurisdictions with a history of voter suppression and intimidation (Brennan Center for Justice 2013). In doing so, the Voting Rights Act eliminated policies and de jure tactics employed to discourage or outright prevent persons of color from voting (e.g., poll taxes, literacy tests, vouchers, etc.). Furthermore, it required that states and jurisdictions that historically engaged in voter suppression and intimidation obtain pre-clearance from the federal government via the Department of Justice prior to implementation (Brennan Center for Justice 2013). Due to incidents in which voting-related material was only provided in English to a population containing a sizable proportion of limited English proficient citizens, the Voting Rights Act also made it illegal to inhibit English-limited citizens from exercising their right to vote (Brennan Center for Justice 2013).

SINCE THE VOTING RIGHTS ACT: CHANGING DEMOGRAPHICS AND THE ELECTORAL COLLEGE

As a result, voting among persons of color, including African-Americans/ blacks specifically, increased exponentially in the years and decades to follow (Sullivan 1999). States where less than one percent of eligible African-Americans were registered to vote prior to the enactment of the Voting Rights Act, witnessed an exponential increase in voter registration among racial and ethnic minorities (Sullivan 1999). The enactment of the Voting Rights Act had ripple effects beyond granting racial and ethnic minorities the right to vote. Because President Lyndon Johnson, a Democrat, publicly endorsed and pushed for the enfranchisement of racial and ethnic minorities, the Democratic Party experienced a mass exodus of southern whites immediately following the enactment of the Voting Rights Act (Caraley 2009). In turn, all of those who departed the Democratic Party became members and loyal supporters of the Republican Party. Their support of the party continues (Tate 1999). Simultaneously, the Democratic Party gained the loyalty and support of black voters. Exit polls in every major election since the enactment of the Voting Rights Act consistently show that the Democratic Party typically garners an overwhelming majority of votes cast by blacks, at times, upward of 90–95 percent (Taylor 2011; Abrajano and Burnett 2012; Caraley 2009). Mirroring its base, politicians and government officials affiliated with the Democratic Party have become increasingly racially and ethnically diverse relative to its counterpart, the Republican Party also known as the Grand Old Party (GOP).

Supporting the findings of the above referenced exit polls, government officials in recent years have confirmed that a record number of votes were cast by African-Americans and Hispanics/Latinos (Taylor and Lopez 2013). A report released by the U.S. Census Bureau in 2013 revealed that the voting participation among racial and ethnic minorities overall has increased gradually each U.S. presidential election since 1996 with the 2012 U.S. presidential election proving to be a record year for African-American voter participation especially (U.S. Census Bureau 2013). Certainly, it is the galvanization of voter support among persons of varying racial and ethnic backgrounds that, without a doubt, contributed to the election (and re-election) of Democratic candidate and now U.S. President, Barack Obama, to two consecutive terms (Cohen 2011; Caswell 2009). Results showed that following the 2008 and 2012 elections the majority of votes in favor of the Democratic candidate were made by persons of diverse races and ethnicities just as they were during the 2000 and 2004 elections (U.S. Census Bureau 2013). Conversely, continuing the trend initiated as a result of the passage of the Voting Rights Act, those who voted for Republican nominees President George W. Bush (2000 and 2004), Senator John McCain (2008), and Governor Mitt Romney

(2012) were overwhelmingly white, male, and older, a demographic that has begun to diverge from the growing diverse American electorate. To gain a better understanding of how demographic changes have potentially impacted the Electoral College, Table 7.1 shows the number of electoral votes cast by each state during the election years of 1992, 2000, 2004, and 2012. It should be noted that the years 1992, 2004, and 2012 were selected in order to allow ample time to detect any population changes, and accordingly, electoral vote allocation that may have occurred during the two decade span as dictated by the 1990, 2000, and 2010 censuses. Electoral data from the 2000 presidential election were provided as additional points of reference during the 20-year time span. Finally, Table 7.1 also shows the political party in receipt of state electoral votes, and consequently, any changes in political party support for each state.

Blue, Red . . . and More Purple

Looking at election years 1992 and 2000, one can easily glean that there were very few, if any, changes in party affiliation in terms of electoral votes cast by the electoral colleges of the 50 states and the District of Columbia. When comparing election years 2004 and 2012, one can effortlessly detect notable changes in the electoral vote counts and/or party support by state. Overall, as illustrative examples, Georgia, North Carolina, South Carolina, and Utah each gained one electoral vote. All three of the states, however, cast their collective electoral votes for the Republican Party, symbolically or colloquially indicated by or referred to as "red." In contrast, a few historically Democratic, or "blue," states lost one or two electoral votes. New York and Pennsylvania, each in possession of a relatively substantial number of electoral votes, lost four and three electoral votes, respectively. On the other hand, California, a historically "blue" state with over 50 electoral votes gained an additional vote helping to compensate, to some degree, for the electoral votes lost by New York and Pennsylvania. Potentially sparking what could be a trend in presidential elections to come, Florida, which voted Republican in the 1992, 2000, and 2004 election years, not only gained additional electoral votes over the 20-year time span, but it also cast its electoral votes for the Democratic candidate in the last two presidential elections. Although not depicted in Table 7.1, Florida was in possession of 27 electoral votes in 2008. In 2012, it was allocated an additional two votes accumulating a total of 29 votes. Political scientists have contended that the current population of Floridians of Cuban descent precisely are now a couple of generations removed from the older, Cuba-born population that has typically supported Republican candidates in the past due to the GOP's platform on U.S. economic sanctions regarding Cuba (Krogstad 2014; Bump 2014).

Comparably, the states of Nevada and Colorado gained electoral votes, and cast their votes in support of the Democratic candidate as well. Interestingly, political scientists posited that the above states' support of the Democratic candidate may be a reflection of the states' growing Hispanic populations. Going a step further, political scientists have also contended that a younger, Hispanic population that connects with what has been described as a more ideologically inclusive party, versus that of the GOP, may also explain to a large degree the shift in support by the Nevada and Colorado constituencies for the Democratic Party (Cohen 2011).

With that in mind, aside from the apparent significance of the number of votes each state possesses and how they cast their votes, the number of electoral votes cast by each state is reflective of the size of the population, or eligible voters, residing within each state. Therefore, as previously mentioned, any changes in the number of electoral votes allocated to a state is without a doubt indicative of changes in the state's population size as determined by the decennial census. Along the same vein, a state's support of a political party in contrast to what it has historically may signify changes in the demographic composition of the state. According to the U.S. Census Bureau, the United States is increasingly becoming a majority-minority country. It is projected that, by the year 2020, those who self-identify as non-Hispanic white will be a part of the racial minority. Growing rates of interracial marriage have contributed to what has been termed "the browning of the U.S. population," as such marital unions are resulting in larger numbers of biracial and multiracial children (Pew Research Center 2013). Evidence of this changing demographic was revealed with the release of 2012 Census data that illustrated slightly more than half of children under the age of one in the year 2011 belonged to a racial or ethnic minority group (U.S. Census Bureau 2012). Thus, it seems that the demographic composition of the U.S. is, in fact, on track to transform into a majority-minority country. As the U.S. population changes in terms of demographics, those who represent it may change accordingly. Although one's race and/or gender may not automatically qualify them to assume leadership roles, once more, social descriptors such as race, gender, class, and so on. individually and cumulatively have a significant impact on one's lived experiences and life chances (Breen 2002). These experiences undoubtedly shape the lens through which social events and issues are interpreted by members of the U.S. population, and voters more pointedly. Therefore, as the racial and ethnic demographics of the collective U.S. population continue to evolve, it would only be logical that the population desire political representation capable of identifying with those issues and events relevant to them.

As an illustration, although Virginia did not gain any electoral votes, unlike the election years of 1992, 2000, and 2004, it cast its 13 electoral votes for

Table 7.1   Electoral Votes by State and Party Affiliation

State	Electoral Vote – 1992 Party	Votes	Electoral Vote – 2000 Party	Vote	Electoral Vote – 2004 Party	Vote	Electoral Vote – 2012 Party	Vote	Net Change 1992–2012
Alabama	Red	9	Red	9	Red	9	Red	9	0
Alaska	Red	3	Red	3	Red	3	Red	3	0
Arizona	Red	8	Red	8	Red	10	Red	11	+3
Arkansas	Blue	6	Red	6	Red	6	Red	6	0
California*	Blue	54	Blue	54	Blue	55	Blue	55	+1
Colorado*,**	Blue	8	Red	8	Red	9	Blue	9	+1
Connecticut	Blue	8	Blue	8	Blue	7	Blue	7	–1
Delaware	Blue	3	Blue	3	Blue	3	Blue	3	0
District of Columbia	Blue	3	Blue	2	Blue	3	Blue	3	
Florida*	Red	25	Red	25	Red	27	Blue	29	+4
Georgia*	Blue	13	Red	13	Red	15	Red	16	+3
Hawaii	Blue	4	Blue	4	Blue	4	Blue	4	0
Idaho	Red	4	Red	4	Red	4	Red	4	0
Illinois	Blue	22	Blue	22	Blue	21	Blue	20	–2
Indiana	Red	12	Red	12	Red	11	Red	11	–1
Iowa	Blue	7	Blue	7	Red	7	Blue	6	–1
Kansas*	Red	6	Red	6	Red	6	Red	6	0
Kentucky	Blue	8	Red	8	Red	8	Red	8	0
Louisiana*	Blue	9	Red	9	Red	9	Red	8	–1
Maine	Blue	4	Blue	4	Blue	4	Blue	4	0
Maryland*	Blue	10	Blue	10	Blue	10	Blue	10	0
Massachusetts*	Blue	12	Blue	12	Blue	12	Blue	11	–1
Michigan	Blue	18	Blue	18	Blue	17	Blue	16	–2
Minnesota	Blue	10	Blue	10	Blue	10	Blue	10	0
Mississippi*	Red	7	Red	7	Red	6	Red	6	–1

State									Change
Missouri	Blue	11	Red	11	Red	11	Red	10	−1
Montana	Blue	3	Red	3	Red	3	Red	3	0
Nebraska	Red	5	Red	5	Red	5	Red	5	0
Nevada*	Blue	4	Red	4	Red	5	Blue	6	+2
New Hampshire	Blue	4	Red	4	Blue	4	Blue	4	0
New Jersey*	Blue	15	Blue	15	Blue	15	Blue	14	−1
New Mexico*	Blue	5	Blue	5	Red	5	Blue	5	0
New York	Blue	33	Blue	33	Blue	31	Blue	29	−4
North Carolina*,**	Red	14	Red	14	Red	15	Red	15	+1
North Dakota	Red	3	Red	3	Red	3	Red	3	0
Ohio**	Blue	21	Red	21	Red	20	Blue	18	−3
Oklahoma*	Red	8	Red	8	Red	7	Red	7	−1
Oregon	Blue	7	Blue	7	Blue	7	Blue	7	0
Pennsylvania**	Blue	23	Blue	23	Blue	21	Blue	20	−3
Rhode Island	Blue	4	Blue	4	Blue	4	Blue	4	0
South Carolina	Red	8	Red	8	Red	8	Red	9	+1
South Dakota	Red	3	Red	3	Red	3	Red	3	0
Tennessee	Blue	11	Red	11	Red	11	Red	11	0
Texas*	Red	32	Red	32	Red	34	Red	38	+6
Utah	Red	5	Red	5	Red	5	Red	6	+1
Vermont	Blue	3	Blue	3	Blue	3	Blue	3	0
Virginia*,**	Red	13	Red	13	Red	13	Blue	13	0
Washington*	Blue	11	Blue	11	Blue	11	Blue	12	+1
West Virginia	Blue	5	Red	5	Red	5	Red	5	0
Wisconsin	Blue	11	Blue	11	Blue	10	Blue	10	−1
Wyoming	Red	3	Red	3	Red	3	Red	3	0
Totals	Blue − 370		Blue − 266		Blue − 251		Blue − 332		
	Red − 168		Red − 271		Red − 286		Red − 206		

* States with at least one county that experienced a documented decrease in non-Hispanic whites since 2000 Census.

** Battleground state.

the Democratic candidate in 2008 and 2012. It is also worth mentioning that 2008 was the first time the Commonwealth of Virginia supported a Democratic presidential candidate since 1968. Because of the striking ideological and political dichotomy that has emerged between the northern and southern parts of the state, Virginia was declared a battleground, or "purple," state leading up to Election Day 2008 and 2012 when it ultimately broke its long-standing pattern and went "blue." This change potentially reflects the increasing demographic diversity among the Virginian electorate. Although voters in the southern portion of the state largely identify as Republican, the denser, northern portion of the state identifies as Democrat and is extremely diverse in terms of race and ethnicity (Lovelace 2015; Vozzella 2014). For instance, within the county of Fairfax, one of the larger counties in northern Virginia, 36 percent of residents identified as non-white in 2014. Among the total population, including those residents who identified as white, approximately 16 percent claimed Hispanic or Latino ethnicity or origins (Economic, Demographic, and Statistical Research 2014). In another example, a 2014 U.S. Census report showed that approximately 21 percent of Prince William County residents identified as black or African-American, a slight increase above the 20 percent calculated during the 2000 Census. More notably, 22 percent of county residents identified as Hispanic or Latino—more than double the nine percent that identified during the 2000 Census (U.S. Census Bureau 2014; U.S. Census Bureau 2000).

Not to be overlooked, results generated as part of the 2010 U.S. Census revealed an almost two percentage point increase among the Asian population within Virginia, as the population steadily approaches six percent of the state. Within Prince William County, eight percent of residents identified as Asian—two percentage points higher than the total state percentage (U.S. Census 2014). A 2009 analysis showed that Asians, who were once Republican loyalists, have heavily voted Democratic Party in the last four presidential elections. Therefore, the higher concentration of Asians within the northern part of the state further solidifies the support of the denser, top part of the state for the Democratic Party.

Similarly, North Carolina, once a solid "red" state, has evolved into a battleground, or "purple," state in recent presidential elections. In 2008, the state, albeit by a narrow margin, voted in support of Democratic candidate, Barack Obama. Four years later, the state narrowly voted in support of the Republican candidate, Mitt Romney at an approximately two percentage point margin (Associated Press 2012). Again, political scientists have attributed the state's change in status to an increasingly racially or ethnically diverse population. Demography statistics released by the Pew Research Center showed that five of North Carolina's once predominantly white counties have shifted to majority-minority counties since 2000 (Krogstad 2015).

According to the Census Bureau, between 2000 and 2010, the percentage of Hispanics in North Carolina virtually doubled from 4.7 to 8.4 (U.S. Census Bureau 2010; U.S. Census Bureau 2000). The African-American, bi-racial, and multiracial populations also experienced slight increases between the 2000 and 2010 census. At the same time, although the number of persons who identified as non-Hispanic whites increased, the proportion of whites comprising the total North Carolina population decreased from 70.2 to 65.3.

It is worth noting that Georgia also gained an additional electoral vote as a result of the recent population growth currently occurring within the state. Demographers have observed that many of those migrating to the state self-identify as black/African-American, Asian, or Hispanic/Latino (Stolberg 2014; U.S. Census Bureau 2014). In 2014, African-Americans comprised approximately 30 percent of the state. In the same year, a little over nine percent self-identified as Hispanic/Latino—almost double the five percent who self-identified as Hispanic/Latino in 2000 (U.S. Census Bureau 2014; U.S. Census Bureau 2010). Those who self-identified as non-Hispanic white made up 54 percent of the state; a substantial decrease from the 66 percent who self-identified as non-Hispanic white in 2000 (U.S. Census Bureau 2014; U.S. Census Bureau 2010). Hence, it is plausible that Georgia, too, may move from the "red" to the "purple" column at some point in the near future.

In viewing Table 7.1, the most stand out figures are the electoral votes totals awarded during the election years of 2000 and 2004. Although the GOP enjoyed victories both years, they were slim victories. Expounding, in 2000, the GOP one by a mere five electoral votes. In 2004, the incumbent enjoyed a more decided victory with 35 more electoral votes than his Democratic challenger. In comparison however, the Democratic candidates have experienced tremendously greater decided victories. In 1992, then Democratic candidate Governor William Clinton won the election by more than 200 electoral votes. In 2012, the Democratic candidate won by more than 100 electoral votes. Though not depicted in the table, the 2008 election resulted in the Democratic candidate winning by 192 electoral votes. Thus, one may reasonably conclude that, relative to the political ideologies and social and economic policies of the Republican Party, the American electorate is increasingly identifying with those policies and ideologies of the Democratic Party.

SHELBY COUNTY V. HOLDER AND OTHER VOTER LAWS

In fact, it is because of the diversity of voter turnout among persons of varying racial and ethnic backgrounds that, according to Chief Justice John Roberts and other members of the majority, the Supreme Court handed down a decision in 2013 that cannot be described as anything less than extraordinary (Savage 2013; Mears and Botelho 2013). Explicitly, in *Shelby County v. Holder*, the Supreme Court declared Section 4 of the Act, which contained a formula that identified precise states and/or locales within the United States with a history of systemic voter suppression based on race, ethnicity, and so on, as unconstitutional. The Court reasoned that, when the formula was initially established, it was during a time of rampant voter suppression, which according to select members of the bench, no longer exists. In its opinion, the Court continued to note that, it is up to the U.S. Congress to update the formula to better suit the current sociopolitical climate and ensure that citizens' right to vote is not abridged based on race, ethnicity, English-speaking capabilities, and so on (Brennan Center for Justice 2013). Notwithstanding, constitutional legal scholars and critics of the ruling have contended that without Section 4 of the Act, Section 5, which requires those states and locales identified under Section 4 to obtain pre-clearance for all new or proposed voting laws from the U.S. Department of Justice prior to enactment or implementation, is consequently all but inconsequential (Brennan Center for Justice 2013; Mann and Wakerman 2013).

Regardless, the *Shelby County v. Holder* decision transpired against a backdrop of accusations of voter fraud from right-wing politicians and pundits. As previously mentioned in Chapter 2, many African-Americans realized a long-held dream with the election of President Barack Obama. Therefore, without a doubt, the 2008 and 2012 U.S. presidential elections will remain indelible entries in the U.S. history books. Aside from African-Americans, many of President Obama's supporters of varying racial and ethnic backgrounds, expressed and displayed indescribable joy ranging from cheers to tears of joy. Just as there were those who were overcome with happiness, there were also those who were less than happy about his historic election and re-election. Many political conservatives and long-time Republicans were displeased out of strict allegiance to their political party affiliation. Others, including both Republican and Democrats alike, were displeased with the results of the historic election and re-election out of pure, racial animus. Some were overt in their displeasure. Some were more covert and elusive, even going so far as to allege voter fraud. As an example, not too long after the 2012 election, there were allegations and speculations of votes cast by non-existent black people in an effort to discredit the authenticity of President Obama's re-election. Charlie Webster, Chair of the Maine Republican Party, in an accusatory tone, openly speculated,

> In some parts of rural Maine, there were dozens, dozens of black people who came in and voted on Election Day. Everybody has a right to vote, but nobody in town knows anyone who's black. How did that happen? I don't know. We're going to find out. (Robillard 2012; Sakuma 2012)

Webster's comments, to a large extent, reflect the overall perception and motivation of political conservatives who were seeking to regain control of the political power structure after President Obama's historic election. Prior to Webster's comments, and in response to the 2008 election of President Obama, the nation witnessed a widespread, dramatic shift with members of the Republican Party suddenly composing the majority among state legislatures and the U.S. House of Representatives as a result of the 2010 mid-term elections (see Chapter 6). Seizing the opportunities provided by the shift in political party composition, state legislatures began proposing voter laws.

Most prominently, attributing their legislative actions to suspicions of voter fraud, and despite revelations that voter fraud occurs on a relatively infrequent basis, a sizable number of Republican-controlled state legislatures set forth new Voter ID laws (Childress 2014; Aleazis, Gilson, and Lee 2012; Weiser and Opsal 2014). Surveillance activities and analyses conducted by government, academic, and non-profit organizations have shown that, voter ID laws ranging in stringency, have increasingly been proposed and enacted by state legislatures since 2000 (i.e., some states mandate identification with a photograph, but other states permit identification without a photograph). Yes, some of the voter laws are a direct result of Help America Vote Act of 2002 (HAVA), a bipartisan effort to improve voter integrity within the United States as a result of the 2000 U.S. presidential election that shed light on ballot issues and potential voter disenfranchisement (Larocca and Klemanski 2011; Walton 2001). Nevertheless, according to the federal independent agency, the General Accounting Office (GAO) and the National Conference of State Legislatures, an undeniable bulk of such laws materialized after the 2010 mid-term elections, with many going in to effect during 2014—the year subsequent to the Supreme Court's ruling in *Shelby County v. Holder* (National Conference of State Legislatures, 2014). Consequently, one could effectively assert that the cumulative effects of the 2010 mid-term elections and *Shelby County v. Holder* have created a political and policy environment ripe for the formation of laws that many perceive as tools of disenfranchisement.

The abundant advent of voter ID laws have unsurprisingly sparked opposition from civil rights organizations and experts. Opponents of voter ID laws suitably contend that such laws discourage, or even prevent, citizens, from exercising one of their fundamental rights. Political scholars have reached conflicting conclusions on the impact of voter ID laws on voter turnout. For example, Larocca and Klemanski determined that the impact of voter ID laws on voter turnout is contingent upon the stringency with which the laws are enforced (2011). Therefore, in order to gain a greater understanding of the impact of voter ID laws on voter turnout, and in response to a Congressional inquiry, the GAO conducted a quasi-experimental study (General Accounting Office 2014). To conduct the study, GAO selected a sample of states with and without voter ID laws. Upon concluding their study, it was determined by investigators that there was indeed a decrease in voter turnout in the two states with voter ID laws as opposed to the remaining, comparative sampled states without similar laws.

Of interest to study investigators, there was also a noticeable difference in the voter turnout rate between whites and blacks, as blacks were less likely to vote in the states with newly implemented voter ID laws. Once more, the findings of the GAO quasi-experimental study affirm the contentions of civil rights organizations such as the National Association for the Advancement of Colored People (NAACP) who voiced concerns about the impact voter ID laws would have on citizens of color and those who have limited English proficiency. In a report prepared by the Brennan Center, it was explicated that persons of color are more likely to encounter difficulties obtaining government-issued ID due to challenges associated with transportation, costs, and, in select rural regions, limited business hours of ID-issuing offices (Gaskins and Sundeep 2012).

In a consonant trend, several states have implemented or proposed laws that eliminate or reduce early voting opportunities. Early voting typically occurs one to two weeks prior to the actual Election Day and has proven to substantially minimize wait times. Thus, like those who oppose voting ID laws, opponents of the elimination or restriction of early voting maintain that such policies serve as an impediment and source of discouragement. Long lines on actual election days typically cause voters to become frustrated and leave polling stations prior to casting their vote. This is of particular concern among older adults who lack the physical stamina to wait in long lines and working persons who may not have the flexibility or paid leave to miss time off of or away from work.

It should be noted that black voters were twice as likely to vote early in Ohio—a state that in recent history has been a key battleground state, successfully selecting the winner of the last 11 U.S. presidential elections. So, it should be of no surprise that those who oppose restricting or eliminating early voting have expressed great trepidation that Ohio, in addition to the 2012 battleground states of Florida, North Carolina, and Wisconsin, have all reduced or eliminated early voting in some manner potentially placing Democratic candidates at a strategic disadvantage considering those voters who cast their ballots early are more likely to vote Democrat, the party that tends to support female and candidates of color (i.e., reduced number of days or terminated night and weekend voting). Because approximately 30 percent of voters cast their ballots early in 2012, reducing or eliminating voting could theoretically detract voters in upcoming national elections from doing so, thereby giving the Republican Party, the party with comparatively minimal number of females and minorities among its ranks, a leg up.

THE EVOLVING ELECTORATE

Regardless of the potential leg up, the lack of diversity among the GOP remains an issue for the party. Although the GOP recently boasted the victorious Mia Love, the first Republican African-American woman elected to the U.S. House of Representatives, she is an anomaly relative to the racial composition of those politicians and elected officials who identify as members of the party. Political party affiliation within U.S. politics has long been determined by race-related issues including civil rights, affirmative action, and so on (Sinclair-Chapman and Price 2008; Sullivan 1999; Tate 1999). As discussed earlier, the role of the Democratic Party in the Voting Rights Act, for instance, won the steadfast support of African-Americans for decades to follow. The Democratic Party's continued left of center support of civil rights issues, in comparison to their largely conservative Republican colleagues, has resulted in a schism largely along racial and ethnic lines. Aside from the obvious reasons a lack of demographic diversity among a political party is problematic for most, changes in the overall social climate within the United States amplifies this predicament.

Millennials

One of the biggest changes is the emergence of the Millennial generation. The Millennial generation, which includes those born between the years of 1981 and 2000, is profoundly different from preceding generations. It is the Millennial generation that is the major catalyst behind the current and ongoing racial and ethnic transformation (Cohen 2011). Pew Center analyses show that the Millennial generation contains a substantial proportion of those who self-identify as African-American/black, Asian, and/or Hispanic with less than 60 percent of Millennials identifying as non-Hispanic whites (Patten 2015). In addition to immigration, Millennials' views of interracial dating and marriage are a primary contributor to the bourgeoning changes in the racial and ethnic make-up of the United States. As an unequivocal indicator, the percent of persons of biracial and multiracial descent are the result of the greater acceptance of interracial relationships among Millennials. There is little question that the United States will continue to alter its collective appearance in the context of race and ethnicity as predicted. In acknowledgment of such changes, one can expect that racial and ethnic minorities will continue to support those candidates that espouse social and political ideologies reflective of their own. More importantly, they will likely continue to support political candidates (and parties) whose ideologies are conducive to the formulation of policies specific to their social and economic interests.

As discussed in Chapter 6, in addition to being more racially and ethnically diverse, the American electorate is better educated than it was a couple of generations ago. Over 50 years ago, the percentage of persons with a bachelor's degree was fairly minimal. At present, the percentage of persons with a bachelor's degree has doubled (U.S. Department of Education 2014). Two generations ago, women were less likely to attend a postsecondary institution. Generation X and Millennial women have pursued, or are pursuing, postsecondary and postgraduate degrees at a far greater rate than women of earlier generations. Women's pursuit of higher education, across all races and ethnicities, has facilitated their widespread entry into the paid labor force in unprecedented numbers. Beginning with Generation X, those born between the years of 1965 and 1980, the percentage of women engaged in the paid labor force began to far outpace women of previous generations, as close to 70 percent are, or have been, members of the paid labor force. Millennial women are seemingly sustaining that trend with over 60 percent in the paid labor force (Patten 2015). Leveraging their greater presence and resulting economic power, women have, quite logically, become engaged in the democratic process by exercising their right to vote at a rate greater than men presumably out of a need to bring attention to those issues of greatest interest to them (e.g., equal pay, reproductive rights, education, healthcare, etc.). Millennial women also tend to be more liberal than their older women counterparts, and therefore more supportive of the Democratic Party (MacManus 2014).

Middle- and Low-Income Classes

Economically, the electorate in its entirety has experienced significant changes. Statisticians, demographers, economists, policy analysts, and so on have all examined, discussed, and/or debated the effects of the housing collapse and resulting recession on the middle class. Consistently, economic and policy experts have concluded that, what was once a booming, stable middle class, is now quite dwindling and vulnerable leaving many of its one-time members to slip into the lower economic rungs. Analyses conducted by the Pew Research Center discovered that four decades ago, 62 percent of individuals or families were considered middle class. However, that proportion has lessened to only 45 percent as of 2011. Also, between the years 2000 and 2010, middle-class wealth decreased by 28 percent (Taylor et al. 2012). It was members of the endangered middle class that helped to elect President Obama in 2008 despite many having reservations about him for reasons ranging from his race to his perceived lack of international policy experience. Responding to the needs of the middle class, President Obama began crafting policies that stymied the markets and stabilize the economy. Policies such as the Affordable Care Act which increased access to care for those with pre-existing conditions and eliminated co-pays for select medications and the Lilly Ledbetter Act which seeks to ensure equal pay for women were part of his administration's efforts to financially steady the middle class. Steps taken by President Obama during the first four years of his presidency helped to win his re-election, as it became clear that, like his Republican colleague Senator John McCain, Governor Mitt Romney was apt to alter or introduce policies that would have benefited the very wealthy while placing the middle class at a continued disadvantage. Furthermore, during several public talks or speeches he gave, it became rather obvious that Governor Romney was out of touch with the needs and interests of those who were not wealthy (Bingham 2012; Stone 2012). Thus, until the middle class and the otherwise economically marginalized obtain a sense of financial security, the electorate may continue to support those candidates sensitive to and motivated by serving the interests of all members of the economic continuum.

CONCLUSION

In the United States' two party system at present, such a candidate is most likely to emerge from the Democratic Party that, relative to the Republican Party, has historically advocated for and/or created those policies that ameliorate the financial burdens disproportionately experienced by low-income and middle-class families. Hence, the politicians and officials within the Democratic Party should reiterate a message of inclusiveness in order to solidify the diversified coalition of voters. With that said, those politicians seeking elected office, including prospective and incumbent women, and women of color, should simultaneously focus, or in many instances, remain focused on strategizing and engaging in the creation of those policies that positively impact racial and ethnic minorities and those disproportionately vulnerable to the changes of the economy and the U.S. labor market. Doing so may increase the likelihood that members of the citizenry will accept and support more members of historically marginalized groups to enter the national political arena. And quite possibly, this will ultimately result in the emergence of a woman, and/or women of color specifically, to the highest executive office.

Chapter 8

Conclusions, Points of Interest, and Recommendations for Future Research

The social markers of race and gender continue to impact politics in the United States. More so, race and gender persist as germane aspects of the national political arena for women and people of color. Although much time has passed since the inception of the American government, navigating the precarious terrain within the entity of electoral politics still proves to be a challenge for women and people of color. Yet, it should be of no surprise that those who are female or a person of color would encounter less than optimal conditions within an entity that was designed by and for white males.

Women have undoubtedly made strides in terms of their representation in the national legislative body. Not long ago, in fact, the United States witnessed the first woman Speaker of the U.S. House of Representatives. Of the 100 U.S. Senators serving in the 114th Congress, 20 are women. That is almost half the total number of women that has served in the U.S. Senate since its genesis (Senate Historical Office). However, just as much has changed, much remains the same considering the number of women who are serving in both houses of the national law making body are vastly disproportionate to the number of women who comprise the general citizenry and American electorate.

The number of people of color serving within both houses is also an underrepresentation of the number of racial and ethnic minorities currently comprising the American electorate. In January 2015, the Pew Research Center released data illustrating that the 114th Congress is the most diverse ever. In the 114th Congress, 17 percent of members are non-white. Of course, this is certainly an increase compared to the 107th Congress where only 12 percent of elected members belonged to a racial or ethnic minority group (Krogstad 2015). However, the 17 percent is still markedly lower than the 38 percent of racial and ethnic minorities that now comprise the American

115

citizenry (Krogstad 2015). To be more pointed, only two of the U.S. Senators serving in the 114th Congress are persons of color—U.S. Senator Corey Booker and U.S. Senator Mazie Hirono (Senate Historical Office).

The historical demographic composition of the national law making body mirrors that of the U.S. Presidency. While the election of a man of color to the U.S. Presidency in 2008 represents some progress, again, there is still much progress to be made.

For women of color, therefore, the road to the U.S. Presidency may prove to be rather unique. The unmistakably exceptional position of black women standing at the intersection of race and gender within the socially manufactured hierarchy is the genesis of black women's tradition of political service and action. On an individual and collective scale, black women have maintained an interest and presence in political spheres. Still, although black women are prevalent political actors within local governments, they are less prevalent among state and national governments (Dittmar 2014). Despite the overall progress of people of color within the United States, women of color, and black women especially, continue to face challenges that impede the increase of their representation in the state and federal governments.

In exploring the 2008 candidacies of now President Barack Obama and then U.S. Senator Hillary Clinton, focus groups with black women from a range of educational and professional backgrounds noted that black women must contend with stereotypes that pervade the public conscience and prevent the perception of black women as competent, levelheaded leaders. While focus group participants conveyed that the election of Barack Obama to the U.S. Presidency is a mark of progress, focus group participants reiterated that black women must contend with systemic, racialized sexism. Therefore, a black woman seeking the U.S. Presidency would have to overcome a somewhat different set of barriers as opposed to now President Barack Obama and then U.S. Senator Hillary Clinton.

Despite their disproportionately low numbers in national government and the barriers they face, black women within the state and national governments, and the national law making body particularly, continue to advocate for women, people of color, and other historically marginalized communities. Whether it is a policy directly impacting women and their families, or legislation that may have an indirect impact on the economic, political, and social aspects of communities of color, the intersecting effects of race and gender remain relevant to the American political arena. Like non-minority women in the U.S. Congress, black women have worked to create or advance those policies and laws that ameliorate social, health, and economic challenges faced by women. However, because social and economic issues related to race and gender reside on a single axis from the standpoint of black women, black women legislators innately view many issues as interrelated, spurring them to act on behalf of women, minorities, and low-income persons and communities (Clawson and Clark 2003).

Their demonstrated willingness and ability to advocate for persons ascribing to multiple identifies is, in fact, an indication of their potential broad appeal if not for the pervasive stereotypes of women, and those specific to black women explicitly, with which they must contend. Reflecting on the open-ended comments provided by survey participants in Chapter 4, while gender stereotypes related to leadership abilities may prevent many from supporting women, stereotypes specific to black women may prevent the galvanizing of broad scale support that would be needed to secure a party nomination at the least (e.g., loud, argumentative, etc.). Nonetheless, as reflected in the results of the 2008 Multi-Racial Post-Election Survey, black women remain committed to the democratic process—and, in some respects, at a greater rate than their women counterparts of other races and ethnicities.

One of the most profound and primary sources of black women's systemic marginalization is the media. The media has consistently and historically played a pivotal role in sustaining prevailing gender norms. In doing so, the media has long portrayed women in roles that are supportive or secondary to men. However, in as much as the media has portrayed women in a fashion that upholds the patriarchal notions of American society, black women have had to contend with the media's construction and reification of stereotypes. Even in the twenty-first century, modern day images of black women in stereotypical roles continue to pervade the social conscience placing black women in a vulnerable and defensive position. For professional black women, this is also the case. Regardless of the educational training, discipline, occupation, position or level of seniority, a consistent theme emerged during interviews with professional black women—the challenge of overcoming racialized and gendered stereotypes while demonstrating their competency and collegiality. Ultimately, interview participants commented that black women pointedly must contend with the prevailing notions of black women as innate mammies and sapphires. Media images of black women in general, as well as those in the political sphere, will likely continue to have an impact on how women of color are perceived. Such images must continue to be challenged by members of the electorate and by those who hold the ear of the public.

Confounding matters is the recent changes in campaign financing. Prior to 2010, fundraising was indeed a challenge for women. Although progress has been made among women politicians, campaign financing remains a daunting notion for many women politicians. Social and professional networks that are typically rife with financial resources and priceless political support and connections also tend to be rife with, and dominated by, white males. Thus, women and minorities have for many years faced barriers to gaining entry to such networks, and consequently, encountered obstacles in generating the tangible and non-tangible resources required to provide support to or launch and sustain an effective, high-stakes campaign. As acknowledged previously, women of color have historically represented marginalized populations and communities including low-income, racial and ethnic minorities, women, and working-class families. Therefore, garnering financial support from such communities or populations probably would not sustain a national campaign. Needless to say the decision of the nation's highest court to lift bans on campaign contributions have created even greater impediments to women and/ or minorities seeking office. As a result, the current political and economic climate that has facilitated an exponential increase in the cost of a national campaign may prove to be even more difficult for a woman of color in pursuit of the Oval Office. Data shared in Chapter 6 illustrated that, in comparison to their black male counterparts, black women seeking elected office in national political offices have been less successful in generating the campaign funds. Therefore, circumventing the impact of *Citizens United* may prove difficult.

The nation's changing demographic, however, may mandate that presidential candidates are reflective of, or at least sensitive to, its needs. The last two U.S. presidential elections have shown that the American electorate is changing racially and ethnically. States that were once solid "red" states have become "purple" reflecting the increasing numbers of minority voters and their respective political, social, and economic needs. Minority populations that once staunchly supported Republican candidates, including Asian and Cuban voters, have begun to support more Democratic candidates. Previously discussed Census analyses revealed that voting participation rates among persons of color are steadily increasing (2013). The increased participation rates of persons of color, and blacks specifically, in elections has helped the Democratic candidate in the last two U.S. presidential elections. Increases in voting among persons of color may be due, in part, to increased levels of educational attainment among citizens of color, as a more educated electorate is more likely to be politically engaged (Berinsky and Lenz 2010). Gender-specific analyses conducted as part of the aforementioned Census study also revealed that black women, who are obtaining postsecondary and postgraduate degrees at a greater rate than previous generations, remain politically active and consistently go to the polls as they have done so historically (Dittmar 2014). They are also more likely than black men to vote. Aside from race, age is an integral factor as well. Younger voters, including Millennial voters, have shown to have diverging political ideologies from that of the Republican Party that is seemingly becoming more and more conservative in terms of women's reproductive rights, financial policies, international relations, and so on. Therefore, someone who can appeal to the social, economic, and political needs of the changing demographic may be embraced if they can overcome the challenges previously outlined.

FIRST AFRICAN-AMERICAN PRESIDENT

Barack Obama, with the help of voters and financial supporters, did what many did not think was possible. He was elected to the U.S. Presidency—twice. There have been many who have critiqued his administration stating that he did little to advance the cause of black people in the United States. In response, there were some who noted that he was not elected to simply represent the cause(s) of one population (Condon and O'Sullivan 2013). He was instead elected to represent a broad spectrum of individuals within the American citizenry. His racial background and experience as a community organizer did, nonetheless, provide him with a unique and intimate understanding of the social and economic ills that exist.

Social and Economic Policies

Upon assuming office, President Obama was faced with a market in virtual free fall accompanied by high rates of unemployment and foreclosures. Simply put, the American economy was on the brink of disaster and on the verge of catapulting many into Depression-like circumstances. Many persons who were demoralized, despondent, and left deprived by the swift changes in the economy were vocal about their discontent. Since taking office, the market has stabilized and unemployment rates have returned to pre-Recession levels. Unemployment rates for racial and ethnic minorities have dropped as well, although they are still higher than those for their white counterparts (Bureau of Labor Statistics 2015). The Affordable Care Act, or Obamacare, was a vital piece of his economic recovery plan, as he stated on multiple occasions that health care was becoming increasingly unaffordable for many families. Obamacare, as detailed in Chapter 2, enables greater access to preventative services thereby emphasizing prevention versus treatment which has proven to be costlier to patients and taxpayers.

In addition to health care reform, other economic policies and reforms were crafted to prevent a repeat of the 2008 financial crisis from happening again. The primary cause of the 2008 financial crisis was the crash of the housing market. Myriad persons who could not afford to buy homes, or large, extravagant homes, were approved to do so. In many instances, however, those who could do so, many of them racial or ethnic minorities, were told that they did not qualify for traditional, low-interest mortgage loans, and instead, were granted variable, high-interest loans (Nier and St. Cyr 2011). Hence, of the most prevalent financial reforms signed into law by President Obama, was the Dodd-Frank Act which established a consumer watchdog to ensure that Americans are not exploited by mortgage lenders. Other components of the legislation include greater restrictions on Wall Street transactions and trading as well as consumer protections against hidden or unexpected bank and credit card fees.

In another example, in an effort to help student loan borrowers obtain some relief, the Obama administration developed the Public Service Loan Program. In essence, the Public Service Loan Program allows borrowers to make payments based on their income for 10 years so long as they remain employed in an occupation that is considered to be of service to the public (e.g., teachers, college professors, civil servant, etc.). Once they have made payments for 10 consecutive years, the loan is then forgiven.

Upon conducting a regression analysis of policies supported by men of color and women during the years 1951 to 2004, Minta and Brown (2014), concluded that men of color in the U.S. House of Representatives have also been integral in the creation of policies that benefit the social and economic welfare of women of all races and ethnicities. According to the authors, due to their interactions with women in the various race and ethnic-specific caucuses within the House, minority men are more likely to be influenced by, and therefore supportive of, women within the caucuses to which they also belong (Minta and Brown 2014). Therefore, the increased diversity within the U.S. House serves to benefit women's issues. For this reason ironically, Minta and Brown contended that the lack of diversity within the U.S. Senate has resulted in less substantive representation of women's issues. Still, although a former U.S. Senator, President Obama has modeled minority men in the U.S. House with his support of women's issues. Making pay equity one of his administration's priorities as mentioned in Chapter 2, on January 2009, President Obama signed his first piece of legislation, the Lilly Ledbetter Fair Pay Restoration Act, making it easier to challenge potential unfair pay based on gender. The act is named after Lilly Ledbetter, a woman who after working for Goodyear Tire & Rubber Company, learned, via an anonymous letter, that she was being paid substantially less than her male counterparts for performing the same job tasks and hours. In total, Ms. Ledbetter accumulated a financial loss of approximately $200,000 in income not including social security benefits and retirement pension (WhiteHouse.gov). Ms. Ledbetter sued the company, won, and was awarded compensatory damages. However, the decision was overturned, as the law existing at that time stated that a suit cannot be filed if the violation occurred more than 180 days before the filing. As a result, the Lilly Ledbetter Act articulates that each discriminatory payment is a separate violation, thereby extending the period of time a person is able to challenge the unfair compensation.

Appointments

Aside from himself, President Obama's cabinet has been rather historic. First, President Obama nominated Lisa Jackson to serve as the Environmental

Protection Agency's Administrator. His nomination made her the first African-American to serve in that post. President Obama also appointed Dr. Susan Rice to serve as the United States' Ambassador to the United Nations, making her the first African-American woman to serve in this position. Outside of his cabinet, President Obama nominated two more women to serve on the United States Supreme Court, one of them being a woman of Hispanic descent. Supreme Court Justice Sonia Sotomayor became the first woman of color to serve on the bench of the nation's highest court upon her confirmation by the U.S. Senate.

Not to be overlooked, President Obama's appointment of Eric Holder to the Office of the U.S. Attorney General was equally historic. As the first African-American U.S. Attorney General, or "top cop," Eric Holder implemented widespread reforms in the criminal justice system. From the beginning of his time as U.S. Attorney General, Holder was outspoken on the racial problems facing America. In concert with his opinions on race, Attorney General Holder made changes to existing policies that had systemically placed vulnerable, low-income and minority populations at a disadvantaged. Of note, he repealed the "three-strikes" policy introduced by the Clinton administration that resulted in the disproportionate incarceration of black, Hispanic, and low-income persons for long periods of time, often for nonviolent offenses. He also fought vigorously against voting laws that adversely impacted the elderly and racial minorities. Eric Holder served in this position throughout Obama's first term and mid-way into his second term. His successor would ultimately be Loretta Lynch, the first African-American woman to serve as the United States Attorney General. Lynch, a Harvard-educated jurist doctorate, who was serving as the U.S. Attorney for the Eastern District of New York at the time of her nomination, has an extensive history of prosecuting terrorists and corrupt police officers, such as those who engaged in the notorious assault of Abner Louima (CNN 2015). Despite her prestigious educational background and impressive work experience, her nomination in November 2014 was met by resistance among members of the U.S. Senate. Her confirmation by the Senate Judiciary Committee took a record five months, more time than it took to confirm the previous Attorney General appointees combined. Congressional committee members and insiders attributed the delay to disputes related to abortion language within the spending bill. However, others attributed the delay to racism and sexism on the part of Congressional members (CNN 2015; Johnson 2015).

CHANGING THE COMPOSITION OF THE NATIONAL ARENA

The appointments made by President Obama are definitely worthy of acknowledgment and a step in the right direction. However, as repeated throughout previous chapters, women, and women of color specifically, remain disproportionately underrepresented in national law making bodies. The lack of representation of representation women and women of color has ripple effects in all sectors of society. Currently only two black women are in leadership positions within the U.S. Congress. Furthermore, because committee assignments within the federal law making body are carried out according to seniority, the small proportion of women and women of color within the legislature decreases the likelihood a sizable number will rise through the ranks, thus preventing them from entering into impactful or influential positions. Consequently, this not only places the populations, communities, and issues for which they advocate at a disadvantage, it also undermines the opportunity to see images of them functioning in roles as competent national leaders addressing a wide range of issues important to a diverse demographic. Because women of color have historically represented majority-minority districts, many assume that they are not capable of representing the interests of a broader demographic.

RACIAL ANIMUS

With the election of President Obama, it was heavily speculated that the country had in fact entered a post-racial era, or a time where race was no longer a central, mitigating factor in terms of human relations or individual life chances. Soon after his election, it was determined that, despite its changing racial and ethnic make-up, America was by no means free of racial prejudice, discrimination, aggression, and/or antagonism. People of all socioeconomic backgrounds expressed ire or disappointment over the election (and re-election) of the first African-American president. Manifestations of racial animus ranged from the lynching of President Obama in effigy by ordinary citizens to the sending and/or distribution of racially offensive jokes about President Obama's familial lineage by sitting judges (Associated Press 2011; Adams 2012).

Other realizations of racial animus have surfaced. As a potent example, in June 2015, Dylan Roof, a young white man, entered into Emanuel African Methodist Episcopal Church in South Carolina and engaged in prayer and Bible study with church members there. After some time, he proceeded to shoot and kill nine of those in attendance (Chuck 2015). It was later learned that Roof's intent was to ignite a race war (Mosendz 2015). Roof's actions came at a time when the country was reeling from a plethora of race-related events that have resulted in the loss of life and/or security among people of color. Since 2012, the shootings of unarmed black men, women, teenagers, and children by police officers and civilians have taken center stage among media outlets (e.g., Laquan McDonald, Trayvon Martin, Jordan Davis, Aiyana Stanley-Jones, Tamir Rice, Rekia Boyd, etc.). Other racially tinged incidents have involved police brutality resulting in the injury and/or death of black men, women, and children (e.g., Eric Garner, Sandra Bland, Samuel Dubose, etc.). The explosion of social media and other technological advances have enabled the audio and visual diffusion of the aforementioned events, sparking social movements to address, and potentially eliminate, the systemic, and at times overt, racial pathology that exists within political, social, and economic institutions (e.g., Black Lives Matter, Say Her Name, etc.).

Of course, the above events are not the only evidence of the racial issues that exist within American society. Examples of racial disparities that persist in almost every segment or aspect of society including health, education, labor, and criminal justice have been outlined to variable degrees above and in preceding chapters.

2016 PRESIDENTIAL ELECTION

Although not a woman, President Barack Obama's administration allowed the national and global community to see a face different from previous presidents, thus changing the face of the norm. His historic presidency may have created a path for another person of color or a woman to the White House. Reflecting on the dwindled group of 2016 presidential hopefuls, that person may be, at the time of this writing, the presumptive Democratic nominee Secretary Hillary Clinton. The Republican field of candidates once again started out as largely white, male, and in support of largely conservative policies including the defunding of Planned Parenthood and the prohibition of certain immigrants from entering the country. The presumptive candidate of the Republican Party, Donald Trump, has made incessant racially charged and misogynistic remarks that have offended many within the demographically changing U.S. population. Meanwhile, the two Democratic candidates, including Secretary Clinton, are again white yet relatively more liberal in terms of their social, political, and economic ideologies and proposed policies.

In order to win the White House and become the first woman Commander-in-Chief, Secretary Clinton will need the support of loyal Democratic voting blocs such as labor unions, teachers, younger adults, and racial and ethnic minorities. Among voters of color, black women continue to be one of the most participatory and loyal voting blocs of the Democratic Party (Pew Research 2015). That is not to say, however, that Secretary Clinton should take for granted that she has the automatic support of black women. In the current social and political climate where racial relations remain at the forefront of television and social media, Secretary Clinton will need to ensure that the issues imperative to communities and women of color would also be issues of priority for her administration.

Of course, the election of the first woman to the White House would actually bring the question of the intersecting realities of race and gender within the context of the presidency full circle. Once again, it would beg the question—has the election of the first African-American president and the election of the first woman as president paved the way for the first African-American woman? Or, as noted previously, could it be the path to the U.S. Presidency for an African-American woman is uniquely contingent upon multiple factors rooted in the reciprocating, historical, systemic, and hegemonic notions of race and gender?

HOW CAN IT BE DONE?

To carve out a successful path, a woman of color could actually, once again, utilize their unique position to craft a successful national campaign. Reflecting on the efforts of women and people of color who have, or are, serving within the political realm, a black woman seeking the U.S. Presidency could very well design an effective strategy. Such a strategy would have to maintain a broad appeal that also generates competitive funding.

Create a Broad, Cross-Cultural Campaign

Although the establishment of majority-minority districts enabled the election of a modest number of black women into a national policy-making body, they have traditionally represented the interests of people who reside within definitive boundaries. The challenges associated with the launch of a national campaign, such as the U.S. Presidency, may require that black women demonstrate and reiterate their ability to represent ethnically, racially, and economically diverse populations. In particular, a black woman seeking the U.S. Presidency should highlight her ability to represent the low-income and middle classes. As the middle class has borne the brunt of recent economic crises, many middle-class persons are unceasingly looking to establish the financial security once held by the American middle class. For example, Congresswoman Alma Adams, representative of North Carolina's 12th District, represents a racially and ethnically diverse district. Although it is deemed a minority-majority district, it is comprised of sizable proportions of whites, African-Americans, and Hispanics of varying income levels (United States Census 2014). Recently, Congresswoman Adams sponsored a bill to aid veterans' small business development, as small businesses serve a vital role in the middle-class economy. Similarly, former Senator Carol Moseley-Braun was elected to the U.S. Senate upon her ability to appeal to a broad array of constituents by focusing on education and gun control—issues still pertinent to many including low-income and middle-class persons regardless of race or ethnicity.

Champion a Hot Button Issue that Impacts Women of All Demographics

Women of color have historically supported and/or represented the interests of those other than persons of color including non-minority women, as discussed in Chapter 2. As an example, former presidential candidate Shirley Chisolm won her congressional seat upon her ability to connect and identify with women and Hispanics as well as blacks (Chisolm 2010). Congresswoman Chisolm took painstaking effort to talk with women of varying racial and ethnic backgrounds in order to ascertain those issues most relevant to them as women and/or mothers. By gaining an in-depth understanding of their needs, she was able to gain their support. Black women politicians must reiterate their long-standing record of representing the interests of a diverse range of persons in order to garner support outside of majority-minority districts.

Leverage Technology

As discussed in Chapter 6 and echoed above, the existing, decidedly exclusive financial and corporate networks are more abundantly composed of white males. These networks are also more likely to support conservative leaning candidates. Coincidentally, candidates supported by these networks are also quite likely to be white and male. With the introduction of the Supreme Court's ruling on campaign finance, raising funds in the national political arena has become an overwhelmingly surreal and ambitious endeavor. In order to circumvent the effects of *Citizens United*, like recent presidential candidates, a black woman candidate would have to initiate and begin a grassroots movement that tapped into an expansive, heterogeneous pool of financial support among a broad range of people. Leveraging technological advances, this could be accomplished via social media and digital donations in the same fashion as President Obama and now presidential candidate, Senator Sanders.

Engage the Younger Generations

Survey results presented in Chapter 4 revealed that younger persons, in comparisons to their older counterparts, maintained a greater sense of optimism in terms of seeing a black woman elected to the U.S. Presidency in their lifetime. Additionally, demographic-related discussions in Chapters 6 and 7 revealed that younger voters hold comparatively liberal stances in terms of their political ideology. Their progressive stances are quite logically a reflection of their perceptions of the changing racial and ethnic demographics within the United States. After all, Generation X and Millennial voters were a formidable force in helping President Obama attain the Democratic Party nomination as well as the U.S. Presidency. Accordingly, it is possible that younger voters could serve as a vital voting block for a candidate who appeals to their social, political, and economic views.

CONCLUSION

The ending of the current presidential administration will mark an end of an era for the United States. The election of Barack Obama to the U.S. Presidency was simply remarkable. His ascent to the U.S. Presidency has left an indelible mark on the memories of those who supported him as well as those he did not. More so, his appointment of highly qualified men and women of color to key judicial and executive branch positions not only helped to change the aesthetics of key offices, it also helped to change the social and political landscape of the country via executive policies and judicial decisions. His election and subsequent re-election could very well be a signal of things to come—more changes in the context of the U.S. Presidency.

If the Democratic nominee, Hillary Clinton, proves to be successful in her bid for the presidency, then the U.S. electorate may well be open to moving forward on a new trajectory from the status quo of middle age white males. A four-year Hillary Clinton administration, most likely followed by an additional four years, would mark 12 (to possibly 16) years the Oval Office would be occupied by someone other than a white male. Now, while 12 years may be a fraction of the total time the U.S. Presidency was held by white males, for younger generations, also known as future voters, they will likely not hold preconceived notions of race and gender in regard to the highest executive office.

To get to the White House, Hillary Clinton will definitely need the support of all persons and groups that have traditionally supported the Democratic Party. One of those groups, or voting blocs, is black women. Given the focus group results revealed in Chapter 3, in which participants indicated that President Obama's election was historically more relevant and exciting than Hillary Clinton's candidacy, it will be interesting to see if Hillary Clinton garners the same level of support from black women. Chances are, even if black women support Hillary Clinton at levels comparable to support of current

President Obama, it will beg the question "are black women supporting her simply out of party loyalty or do they really believe as a woman she will represent their best interests?" Re-occurring racially tinged conflicts that result in the severe injury or death of minority men, women, and children is a priority for many black women who have had to bury their sons, daughters, husbands, and so on. Therefore, Clinton will need to appeal to this traditional voting bloc with policy proposals that seek to minimize or halt such incidents. Further research, time, and observation will be required to probe this question.

If elected, it will also be interesting to watch how Clinton assembles her cabinet. First, it will be interesting to see if her cabinet is reflective of the country's overall gender composition or, in an attempt to assuage the fears of those who still ascribe to traditional gender norms, a mirror reflection of the national legislative bodies that are heavily male. Even if Clinton's cabinet reflects the gender composition of the U.S. population, will her cabinet and top advisors also incorporate the racial and ethnic composition of the country? If it in fact does, then her cabinet or top advisors should then include a visible number of women of color. This again would allow the country to see more women of color, and black women in particular, in leadership roles and help to diminish the stereotypical perceptions with which many professional black women, and black women politicians as well, must contend.

Bibliography

Abraham, L. and O. Appia. 2006. "Framing News Stories: The Role of Visual Imagery in Priming Racial Stereotypes." *Howard Journal of Communications* 17: 183–203.

Abrajano, Marisa and Craig Burnett. 2012. "Do Blacks and Whites See Obama through Race-Tinted Glasses?: A Comparison of Obama's and Clinton's Approval Ratings." *Presidential Studies Quarterly* 42(2):363–75.

Abrams, Jim. 2011. "House Ethics Committee Releases Three Counts of Alleged Ethics Violations against Maxine Waters," *Huffintgon Post*, August 9 (http://www. huffingtonpost.com/2010/08/09/house-ethics-committee-ch_n_675680.html).

Adams, John. 2012. "Federal Judge Who Sent Racist Obama E-mail Requests Review." *USA Today*, March 1 (http://usatoday30.usatoday.com/news/nation/ story/2012-03-01/montana-judge-racist-email-obama/53325420/1/).

Adoni, H. and S. Mane. 1984. "Media and the Social Construction of Reality: Toward an Integration of Theory and Research." *Communication Research* 11:323–40.

Adkins, Randall and Andrew Dowdle. 2002. "The Money Primary: What Influences the Outcome of Pre-Primary Presidential Nomination Fundraising?" *Presidential Studies Quarterly* 32(2):256–75.

Aguiar, Marian. 1999. "Montgomery Bus Boycott." Pp. 1328–30 in *Africana: The Encyclopedia of the African and African American Experience*, edited by K. A. Appiah and H. L. Gates. New York, NY: Basic Civitas Books.

Airhihenbwa, Collins, J. Dewitt Webster, and Titilayo Oladosu. 2004. "Transforming Structural Barriers to Improve the Health of African Americans." Pp. 792–807 in *Praeger Handbook of Black American Health: Policies and Issues Behind Disparities in Health,* edited by I. Livingston.

Aleazis, Hamed, Dave Gilson, and Jaeah Lee. 2012. "UFO Sightings Are More Common Than Voter Fraud,." *Mother Jones*, July/August (http://www.motherjones. com/politics/2012/07/voter-id-laws-charts-maps).

Allen, Jonathan and Bresnahan, John. 2010. Decision Near on Maxine Waters Ethics Case. *Politico*, July 29 (http://www.politico.com/news/stories/0710/40399.html).

American Association of University Women. 2014. *By the Numbers: A Look at the Gender Pay Gap*. Washington, DC: American Association of University Women. Retrieved March 1, 2015 (http://www.aauw.org/2014/09/18/gender-pay-gap/).

Anderson-Bricker, Kristin. 1999. "'Triple Jeopardy': Black Women and the Growth of Feminist Consciousness in SNCC, 1964–1975." Pp. 49–69 in *Still Climbing, Still Lifting: African American Women's Contemporary Activism*, edited by Kimberly Springer. New York: New York University Press.

Andrews, Helena. 2007. Hillary and the Giant Peach. *Politico*, July 24 (http://www.politico.com/story/2007/07/hillary-and-the-giant-peach-005087).

Angelou, Maya. 1994. *The Complete Collected Poems of Maya Angelou*. New York, NY: Random House.

Alex-Assensoh, Yvette. 2008. "Change and the 2008 American Presidential Election." *Politicka Misao: Croatian Political Science Review* 45(5):235–43.

Arcenueaux, Kevin. 2001. "The 'Gender Gap' in State Legislative Representation: New Data to Tackle an Old Question." *Political Research Quarterly* 54(1):143–60.

Associated Press. 2011. "Obama Effigy Hung in Rhode Island School that Fired All Its Teachers." *Huffington Post*, May 18 (http://www.huffingtonpost.com/2010/03/18/obama-hung-in-effigy-at-r_n_504746.html).

Associated Press. 2012. "2012 North Carolina Presidential Results." *Politico*, November 19 (http://www.politico.com/2012-election/results/president/north-carolina/).

Ayers, Bill and Bernadine Dohrn,. 2009. "What Race Has to Do With It." *Monthly Review* 60(10) (http://www.monthlyreview.org/090316ayers-dohrn.php).

Baker, Andy and Corey Cook. 2005. "Representing Black Interests and Promoting Black Culture: The Importance of African American Descriptive Representation in the U.S. House." *DuBois Review* 2(2):227–245.

Barrett, Edith. 1995. "The Policy Priorities of African American Women in State Legislatures." *Legislative Studies Quarterly* 20(2):223–47.

Bay, Mia. 2010. *To Tell the Truth Freely: The Life of Ida B. Wells*. New York, NY: Hill and Wang.

Bendery, Jennifer. 2012. "Trayvon Martin Resolution Introduced by Congressional Black Caucus." *Huffington Post*, April 4 (http://www.huffingtonpost.com/2012/04/04/trayvon-martin-resolution-congressional-black-caucus_n_1404441.html).

Benedetto, Richard. 2005. "GOP: 'We Were Wrong' to Play Racial Politics." *USA Today*, July 14 (http://www.usatoday.com/news/washington/2005-07-14-GOP-racial-politics_x.htm).

Berberoglu, Berch. 1998. *An Introduction to Classical and Contemporary Social Theory: A Critical Perspective, Second Edition*. New York: General Hall.

Berger, C. 2000. "Quantitative Depictions of Threatening Phenomena in News Reports: The Scary World of Frequency Data." *Human Communications Research* 26:27–52.

Berinsky, Adam and Gabriel Lenz. 2010. "Education and Political Participation: Exploring the Causal Link." *Political Behavior* 33:357–73.

Bingham, Amy. 2012. "Is Mitt Romney Out of Touch?" *ABC News*, February 27 (http://abcnews.go.com/Politics/OTUS/mitt-romney-touch/story?id=15801839).

Birzee, Michael and Jackquice Smith-Mahdi, 2006. "Does Race Matter? The Phenomenology of Discrimination Experienced among African-Americans." *Journal of African-Americans* 10(2):22–37.

Bjornstrom, E., R. L. Kaufman, R. D. Peterson, and M. D. Slater. 2010. "Race and Ethnic Representations of Lawbreakers and Victims in Crime News: A National Study of Television Coverage." *Social Problems* 57:269–93.

Black, Angela and Nadine Peacock. 2011. "Pleasing the Masses: Messages for Daily Life Management in African American Women's Popular Media Sources." *American Journal of Public Health* 101(1):144–50.

Boonstra, Heather and Elizabeth Nash. 2014. *A Surge of State Abortion Restrictions Puts Providers—and the Women They Serve-in the Crosshairs*. Washington, DC: Guttmacher Institute. Retrieved August 2015 (http://www.guttmacher.org/pubs/gpr/17/1/gpr170109.pdf).

Branch, Taylor. 1988. *Parting the Waters: America in the King Years, 1954–1963*. New York, NY: Simon and Schuster, Inc.

Bratskeir, Anne. 2009. "Hillary Clinton Pantsuit Saga Continues." *Newsday*, August 11 (http://www.newsday.com/long-island/politics/hillary-clinton-s-pantsuit-saga-continues-1.1363380).

Breen, Richard. "A Weberian Approach to Class Analysis." in *Alternative Foundations of Class Analysis*, edited by Erik Olin Wright. New York: Cambridge University Press.

Brennan Center for Justice. 2013. *Shelby County v. Holder (Amicus Brief)*. New York, NY: Brennan Center for Justice. Retrieved June 10, 2015 (http://www.brennancenter.org/legal-work/shelby-county-v-holder-amicus-brief).

Bresnahan, John. 2012. "Waters ethics case debacle detailed." *Politico*, September 25 (http://www.politico.com/story/2012/09/report-details-waters-ethics-case-debacle-081665).

Brown, Matthew. 2014. "Groups Want to See Montana Judge's Racist Obama Email." *Huffington Post*, July 2 (http://www.huffingtonpost.com/2014/07/02/montana-judge-racist-obama-email_n_5552853.html).

Bump, Philip. 2014. "The Politics of the Increasingly Democratic Cuban Vote." *The Washington Post*, December 17 (https://www.washingtonpost.com/news/the-fix/wp/2014/12/17/the-politics-of-the-increasingly-democratic-cuban-vote/).

Bureau of Labor Statistics. 2015. *Labor Force Statistics from the Current Population Survey*. Washington, DC: United States Department of Labor. Retrieved July 14, 2015 (http://data.bls.gov/pdq/SurveyOutputServlet).

Bureau of Labor Statistics. 2014. *Women in the Labor Force: A Databook*. Washington, DC: United States Department of Labor. Retrieved July 28, 2015 (http://www.bls.gov/opub/reports/cps/women-in-the-labor-force-a-databook-2014.pdf).

Bureau of Labor Statistics. 2016. *Usual Weekly Earnings of Wage and Salary Workers Fourth Quarter 2015*. Washington, DC: United States Department of Labor. Retrieved February 15, 2016 (http://www.bls.gov/news.release/pdf/wkyeng.pdf).

Burrell, Barbara. 2006. "Looking for Gender in Women's Campaigns for National Office in 2004 and Beyond: In What Ways is Gender Still a Factor?" *Politics & Gender* 2(3):354–59.

Burton, Vernon. 1978. "Race and Reconstruction: Edgefield County, South Carolina." *Journal of Social History* 12(1):31–56.

Bystrom, D. G., T. A. Robertson, and M. C. Banwart. 2001. "Framing the Flight: An Analysis of Media Coverage of Female and Male Candidates in Primary Races for Governor and U.S. Senate in 2000." *American Behavioral Scientist* AA (2):1999–2013.

Callahan, V. 2012. "Media Consumption, Perceptions of Crime Risk, and Fear of Crime: Examining Race/Ethnic Differences." *Sociological Perspectives* 55:93–115.

Campo-Flores, Ariana. 2012. "Cuban-Americans Move Left." *The Wall Street Journal*, November 8 (http://www.wsj.com/articles/SB10001424127887324073504578107412795405272)

Caraley, Demetrios James. 2009. "Three Trends Over Eight Presidential Elections, 1980–2008: Toward the Emergence of a Democratic Majority Realignment?" *Political Science Quarterly* 124(3):423–42.

Carpenter, T. 2012. "Construction of the Crack Mother Icon." *Western Journal of Black Studies* 36:264–75.

Carroll, Susan and Richard Fox. 2014. *Gender and Elections: Shaping the Future of American Politics 3rd Edition.* New York, NY: Cambridge University Press

Carroll, Susan and Ronnee Schreiber. 1997. "Media coverage of women in the 103rd Congress." In *Women, Media, and Politics* edited by. P. Norris. New York, NY: Oxford University Press.

Cash, T. F. and P. E. Henry. 1995. "Women's Body Images: The Results of a National Survey in the USA." *Sex Roles* 33: 19–28.

Caswell, Bruce. 2009. "The presidency, the Vote, and the Formation of New Coalitions." *Polity* 41(3):388–407.

Celis, Karen. 2012. "On Substantive Representation, Diversity and Responsiveness." *Politics & Gender* 8(4): 524–29.

Center for American Women and Politics. 2015. Current Numbers. Rutgers, NJ: Rutgers Eagleton Institute of Politics. Retrieved April 2015 (http://www.cawp.rutgers.edu/current-numbers).

Chang, Ailsa. 2014. *From Humble Beginnings, A Powerhouse Fundraising Class Emerges.* Washington, DC: National Public Radio. Retrieved June 15, 2015 (http://www.npr.org/2014/05/06/310134589/from-humble-beginnings-a-powerhouse-fundraising-class-emerges).

Childress, Sarah. 2014. *Why Voter ID Laws Aren't Really about Fraud.* Arlington, VA: Public Broadcasting Station. Retrieved August 29, 2015 (http://www.pbs.org/wgbh/frontline/article/why-voter-id-laws-arent-really-about-fraud/).

Chisolm, Shirley. 2010. *Unbought and Unbossed: 40th Anniversary Edition.* New York, NY: Take Root Media.

Chozick, Amy. 2015. "Hillary Clinton Announces 2016 Presidential Bid." *The New York Times*, April 12 (http://www.nytimes.com/2015/04/13/us/politics/hillary-clinton-2016-presidential-campaign.html?_r=0).

Chuck, Elizabeth. 2015. "Charleston Church Shooter Dylann Roof 'Caught Us With Our Eyes Closed.'" *NBC News*, September 10 (http://www.nbcnews.com/storyline/charleston-church-shooting/charleston-church-survivors-shooter-caught-us-our-eyes-closed-n424331).

Cillizza, Christopher. 2010. "Majority Leader Reid Apologizes to Obama for 2008 Remarks." *The Washington Post*, January 10 (http://www.washingtonpost.com/ wp-dyn/content/article/2010/01/09/AR2010010902141.html).

Clawson, Rosalee and John A. Clark. 2003. "The Attitudinal Structure of African American Women Party Activists: The Impact of Race, Gender, and Religion." *Political Research Quarterly* 56(2):211–21.

Clinton, Catherine. 2005. *Harriet Tubman: The Road to Freedom.* New York, NY: Back Bay Books.

Cohen, Cathy. 2011. "Millenials & the Myth of the Post-Racial Society: Black Youth, Intra-Generational Divisions & the Continuing Racial Divide in American Politics." *Daedalus* 140(2):197–205.

Comden, Betty, Green, Adolph, and Styne, Julie. 1963. *Now!*

Condon Jr., George and Jim O'Sullian. 2013. "Has President Obama Done Enough for Black Americans?" *The Atlantic*, April 5 (http://www.theatlantic.com/ politics/archive/2013/04/has-president-obama-done-enough-for-black-americans/ 274699/).

Condon, Stephanie. 2010. "Maxine Waters to Face Ethics Trial." *CBS News*, August 2 (http://www.cbsnews.com/8301–503544_162–20012335–503544.html).

Congressional Office of History and Preservation, Office of the Clerk. 2014. *Women of Color in Congress.* Washington, DC: US Government Printing Office. Retrieved October 6, 2015 (http://history.house.gov/Exhibitions-and-Publications/ WIC/Historical-Data/Women-of-Color-in-Congress/).

Congressional Office of History and Preservation, Office of the Clerk. 2014. *Women Representatives and Senators by Congress, 1917-Present.* Washington, DC: US Government Printing Office. Retrieved October 7, 2015 (http://womenincongress. house.gov).

Congressional Office of History and Preservation, Office of the Clerk. n.d. *Carol Moseley Braun.* Washington, DC: U.S. House of Representatives. Retrieved January 22, 2015 (http://history.house.gov/People/Detail?id=18611).

Conley, Dalton. 2001. "Being Black, Living in the Red: Wealth Matters." in *Race, Class, and Gender in the United States. 5th Edition*, edited by P. S. Rothenberg. New York: Worth Publishers

Crenshaw, Kimberle. 2000. "Demarginalizing the Intersection of Race and Sex: A Black Feminist Critique of Antidiscrimination Doctrine, Feminist Theory and Antiracist Policies" in *The Black Feminist Reader*, edited by J. James and T. Denean Sharpley-Whiting. Malden, MA: Blackwell Publishers.

Crespin, Michael H. and Janna Deltz. 2010. "If You Can't Join 'em, Beat 'em: The Gender Gap in Individual Donations to Congressional Candidates." *Political Research Quarterly* 63(3):581–93.

Dallek, Robert. 2003. *An Unfinished Life: John F. Kennedy.* New York, NY: Back Bay Books.

Darcy, R. and Charles Hadley. 1987. "Black Women in Politics: The Puzzle of Success." *Social Science Quarterly* 629:645.

deCoteau, N., K. Jamieson, K., and D. Romer. 1998. "The Treatment of Persons of Color in Local Television News: Ethnic Blame Discourse or Realistic Group Conflict?" *Communication Research* 25:286–98.

Dedman, Bill. 2001. "Study Discerns Disadvantages for Blacks in Home Mortgages." in *Race, Class, and Gender in the United States. 5th Edition*, edited by P. S. Rothenberg. New York: Worth Publishers.

Department of Neighborhood and Community Services. 2014. *Demographic Reports 2014: County of Fairfax, Virginia. Economic, Demographic, and Statistical Research*.

Dickerson, Bette, Wanda Parham-Payne, and Tekisha D. Everette. 2012. "Single Mothering in Poverty: Black Feminist Considerations." Pp. 91–111 in Social Production and Reproduction at the Interface of Public and Private Spheres (*Advances in Gender Research*), edited by Marcia Texler Segal, Esther Ngan-Ling Chow, and Vasilike Demos. United Kingdom: Emerald Publishing.

Dittmar, Kelly. 2014. *Voices. Votes. Leadership.: The Status of Black Women in Politics*. New Brunswick, NJ: Center for American Women and Politics. Retrieved May 5, 2015 (http://www.cawp.rutgers.edu/sites/default/files/resources/hh2015.pdf).

Dittmar, Kelly. 2012. *What Role Will Women Play in the Legislative Debate Over Gun Control?* Brunswick, NJ: Center for American Woman and Politics. Retrieved May 5, 2015 (http://cawp.rutgers.edu/footnotes/what-role-will-women-play-in-the-legislative-debate-over-gun-control).

Dolan, Kathleen. 2005. "Do Women Candidates Play to Gender Stereotypes?: Do Men Candidates Play to Women? Candidate Sex and Issues Priorities on Campaign Websites." *Political Research Quarterly* 58(1):31–44.

Dolan, Kathleen. 2014. "Gender Stereotypes, Candidate Evaluations, and Voting for Women: What Really Matters?" *Political Research Quarterly* 67(1):96–107.

DuBois, W. E. B. 1935. *The Black Codes*.

Eargle, Lisa, Ashraf Esmail, and Jas Sullivan. 2008. "Voting the Issues or Voting the Demographics? The Media's Construction of Political Candidates' Credibility." *Race, Gender & Class* 15(3/4):8–21.

Eberhardt, Jennifer. 2010. "Enduring Racial Associations: African Americans, Crime, and Animal Imagery." Pp. 439–57 in *Doing Race: 21 Essays for the 21st Century*, edited by H. R. Marcus and P. Moya. New York, NY: W. W. Norton.

Edghill, Vernese. 2007. "Black Women in Race-Specific Positions on Predominantly White Campuses: A Historical Materialist Analysis" Ph.D. Dissertation, Department of Sociology and Anthropology, Howard University.

Edwards, Donna. "Introduced Legislation." *House.gov* (http://donnaedwards.house.gov/index.php?option=com_content&view=article&id=407&Itemid=31).

Eggen, Dan. 2012. "Obama Fundraising Powered by Small Donors, New Study Shows." *The Washington Post*, February 8 (https://www.washingtonpost.com/politics/obama-fundraising-powered-by-small-donors-new-study-shows/2012/02/08/gIQANfKIzQ_story.html).

Eschholz, S., T. Chiricos, and M. Gertz. 2003. "Television and Fear of Crime: Program Types, Audience Traits, and the Mediating Effect of Perceived Neighborhood Racial Composition." *Social Problems* 50:395–415.

Falk, Erika. 2010. *Women for President: Media Bias in Nine Campaigns, 2nd Edition*. Chicago, IL: University of Illinois Press.

Farganis, James. 2000. *Readings in Social Theory: The Classic Tradition to Post-Modernism*. New York, NY: McGraw-Hill.

Feldman, Marcus. 2010. "The Biology of Ancestry: DNA, Genomic Variation, and Race." Pp. 136–59 in *Doing Race: 21 Essays for the 21st Century*, edited by H. R. Marcus and P. Moya. New York, NY: W. W. Norton.

Feldstein, Ruth. 2013. *How it Feels to be Free: Black Women Entertainers and the Civil Rights Movement*. New York, NY: Oxford University Press.

Flock, Elizabeth. 2012. "Birth Control Hearing on Capitol Hill Had Mostly Male Panel of Witnesses." *The Washington Post*, February 16 (https://www.washingtonpost.com/blogs/blogpost/post/birth-control-hearing-on-capitol-hill-had-all-male-panel-of-witnesses/2012/02/16/gIQA6BM5HR_blog.html).

Ford, Lynne. 2011. *Women & Politics: The Pursuit of Equality*. Boston, MA: Cengage Learning, Forner, Eric. 2002. *Reconstruction: America's Unfinished Business*. New York, NY: HarperCollins.

Fox, Richard and Jennifer Lawless. 2014. "Uncovering the Origins of the Gender Gap in Political Ambition." *American Political Science Review* 108(3):499–519.

Freeman Gill, John. 2008. "Cold Shoulders." *The New York Times*, July 27 (http://www.nytimes.com/2008/07/27/nyregion/thecity/27harl.html?pagewanted=all&_r=0).

Fulton, Sarah. 2012. "Running Backwards and in High Heels: The Gendered Quality Gap and Incumbent Electoral Success." *Political Research Quarterly* 65(2):303–14.

Gaddis, S. Michael. 2014. "Discrimination in the Credential Society: An Audit Study of Race and College Selectivity in the Labor Market." *Social Forces* 93(4):1451–79.

Garfield, G. 2007. "Hurricane Katrina: The Making of Unworthy Victims." *Journal of African American Studies* 10(4):55–74.

Gaskins, Keesha and Iyer Sundeep. 2012. The Challenges of Obtaining Voter Identification. New York, NY: Brennan Center for Justice. Retrieved September 2015 (http://www.brennancenter.org/sites/default/files/legacy/Democracy/VRE/Challenge_of_Obtaining_Voter_ID.pdf).

Gateward, Fraces. 1999. "Documenting the Struggle: African American Women as Media Artists, Media Activists." Pp. 275–96 in *Still Climbing, Still Lifting: African American Women's Contemporary Activism* edited by Kimberly Springer. New York: New York University Press.

General Accounting Office. September 2014. Elections: Issues Related to State Voter Identification Laws. GAO-14–634.

Gerbner, G., M. Morgan, and N. Signorielli. 1982. "Programming Health Portrayals: What Viewers See, Say, and Do." Pp. 291–307 in *Television and Behavior: Ten Years of Scientific Progress and Implications for the '80s*, Vol. 2, edited by D. Pearl, J. Lazar, and L. Bouthilet. Washington, DC: U.S. General Printing Office.

Gershon, Sarah. 2012. "When Race, Gender, and the Media Intersect: Campaign News Coverage of Minority Congresswomen." *Journal of Women, Politics, and Policy*. 33(2):105–25.

Gibbs, Nancy and Michael Scherer. 2009. Up Close. *Time* 173(21):26–33.

Giddings, Paula. 2006. *When and Where I Enter: The Impact of Black Women on Race and Sex in America*. New York, NY: Amistad.

Griffin, John, D. and Michael Keane. 2011. "Are African Americans Effectively Represented in Congress?" *Political Research Quarterly* 64(1):145–56.

Gupta, Prachi. 2014. "People Magazine Deletes Racist Tweet about Viola Davis." *Salon*, September 26 (http://www.salon.com/2014/09/26/people_magazine_ deletes_racist_tweet_about_viola_davis/).

Guttmacher Institute. 2015. *In Just the Last Four Years, States Have Enacted 231 Abortion Restrictions*. Retrieved May 2015 (http://www.guttmacher.org/media/ inthenews/2015/01/05/).

Hamburger, Tom and Matea Gold. 2015. "Jeb Bush, meeting with Potential Donors, Looks to Draw Contrast with Romney." *The Washington Post*, January 21 (https:// www.washingtonpost.com/news/post-politics/wp/2015/01/20/jeb-bush-meets-with-potential-donors-in-dc/).

Hanson, Joyce. 2003. *Mary McLeod & Black Women's Political Activism*. Columbia, MO: University of Missouri Press.

Hardaway, C. and V. McLoyd. 2009. "Escaping Poverty and Securing Middle-Class Status: How Race and Socioeconomic Status Shape Mobility Prospects for African Americans During the Transition to Adulthood." *Journal of Youth & Adolescence* 38(2):242–56.

Harris, David. 1999. "The Stories, the Statistics and the Law: Why 'Driving While Black' Matters." *Minnesota Law Review* 84:265–326.

Harris-Perry, Melissa. 2011. *Sister Citizen: Shame, Stereotypes, and Black Women in America*. New Haven, CT: Yale University Press.

Harrison, Robert. 2006. "From Biracial Democracy to Direct Rule: The End of Self-Government in the Nation's Capital, 1865–1878." *Journal of Policy History* 18(2):241–69.

Hauslohner, Abigail. 2016. "Former D.C. Mayor Vincent Gray to Run for Ward 7 Council Seat." Washington Post, February 4 (https://www.washingtonpost.com/ local/dc-politics/former-dc-mayor-vincent-gray-to-run-for-ward-7-city-council-seat/2016/02/04/4220195a-caaa-11e5-ae11-57b6aeab993f_story.html).

Hayden, Grant. 2004. "Resolving the Dilemma of Minority Representation." *California Law Review* 92(6):1589–637.

Hee Lee, Michelle Ye. 2015. "Does Obamacare Provide Federal Subsidies for Elective Abortions?" *The Washington Post*, January 26 (http://www.washingtonpost. com/blogs/factchecker/wp/2015/01/26/does-obamacare-provide-federal-subsidies-for-elective-abortions/).

Heinberg, L. J. and J. K. Thompson. 1995. "Body Image and Televised Images of Thinness and Attractiveness: A Controlled Laboratory Investigation." *Journal of Clinical Psychology* 14:325–38.

Helderman, Rosalind S. 2012. "California Representative Waters Cleared of Ethics Charges." *The Washington Post*, September 21 (http://www.washingtonpost.com/ blogs/2chambers/post/maxine-waters-cleared-of-house-ethics-charges/2012/09/21/ 75d346c2–03f3–11e2–8102-ebee9c66e190_blog.html).

Henkel, Kristin, John Dovidio, and Samuel Gaertner. 2006. "Institutional Discrimination, Individual Racism, and Hurricane Katrina." *Analyses of Social Issues and Public Policy* 6(1):99–124.

Heppen, John. 2003. "Racial and Social Diversity and U.S. Presidential Election Regions." *Professional Geographer* 55(2):191–205.

Hill-Collins, Patricia. 2000. *Black Feminist Thought*. New York, NY: Routledge Press.

hooks, bell. 2000. *Feminist Theory: From Margin to Center.* Cambridge, MA: South End Press.

Institute for Women's Policy Research. 2015. *The Status of Women in the United States.*" Washington, DC: Institute for Women's Policy Research. Retrieved September 2015 (http://statusofwomendata.org/explore-the-data/political-participation/political-participation-full-section/#ppintroduction).

Iyengar, Shanto. 1989. "How Citizens Should Think About National Issues: A Matter of Responsibility." *American Journal of Political Science* 33:878–900.

Iyengar, Shanto. 2010. "Race in the News: Stereotypes, Political Campaigns, and Market-Based Journalism." Pp. 251–73 in *Doing Race: 21 Essays for the 21st Century,* edited by H. R. Marcus and P. Moya. New York, NY: W. W. Norton.

Jeffries, Judson. 1999. "U.S. Senator Edward W. Brooke and Governor L. Douglass Wilder Tell Political Scientists How Blacks Can Win High-Profile Statewide Office." *PS: Political Science & Politics* 32(3):583–87.

Jeffries, Judson and Charles Jones. 2006. "Blacks Who Run for Governor and the U.S. Senate: An Examination of their Candidacies." *Negro Educational Review* 57(3/4):243–65.

Jenkins, Shannon. 2007. A Woman's Work is Never Done?: Fund-Raising Perception and Effort Among Female State Legislative Candidates. *Political Research Quarterly* 60(2):230–39.

Jeydal, Alana and Andrew Taylor. 2003. "Are Women Legislators Less Effective?: Evidence from the U.S. House in the 103rd–105th Congress." *Political Research Quarterly* 56(1):19–28.

Johnson, Theodore. 2015. "The Political Power of the Black Sorority." *The Atlantic,* April 26 (http://www.theatlantic.com/politics/archive/2015/04/loretta-lynch-and-the-political-power-of-the-black-sorority/391385/).

Jones, Althena. 2015. "Loretta Lynch Makes History." *Cable News Network,* April 27 (http://www.cnn.com/2015/04/23/politics/loretta-lynch-attorney-general-vote/.

Jones, Joyce. October 5, 2010. "Community College Summit to Highlight Initiatives, Promote New Ideas." Diverse Education.

Kahn, Kim. 1996. *The Political Consequences of Being a Woman.* New York, NY: Columbia University Press.

Kaiser Family Foundation. 2013. *The Public's Health Care Agenda for the 113th Congress.* Washington, DC: Kaiser Family Foundation. Retrieved May 2015 (http://kff.org/report-section/methodology-publics-health-care-agenda-for-the-113th-congress/).

Kentor, Jeffrey and Yong Suk Jang. 2004. "Yes, There is a (Growing) Transnational Business Community: A Study of Global Interlocking Directorates 1983–1998." *International Sociology* 19(3):355–68.

Klein, R. 2003. "Audience Reactions to Local TV News." *The American Behavioral Scientist* 46:1661–72.

Krogstad, Jens Manuel. 2014. *After Decades of GOP Support, Cubans Shifting Towards the Democratic Cuban Party.* Washington, DC: Pew Research Center. Retrieved July 18, 2015. http://www.pewresearch.org/fact-tank/2014/06/24/after-decades-of-gop-support-cubans-shifting-toward-the-democratic-party/.

Krogstad, Jens Manuel. 2014. *Reflecting A Racial Shift, 78 Counties Turned Majority Since 2000.* Washington, DC: Pew Research Center. Retrieved July 18, 2015 (http://www.

pewresearch.org/fact-tank/2015/04/08/reflecting-a-racial-shift-78-counties-turned-majority-minority-since-2000/).

Larocca, Roger and John Klemanski. 2011. "U.S. State Election Reform and Turnout in Presidential Elections." *State Politics & Policy Quarterly* 11(1):76–101.

LaVeist, T., D. J. Gaskins, and P. Richard. 2009. *The Economic Burden of Health Inequalities in the United States.* Washington, DC: The Joint Center for Political and Economic Studies. Retrieved May 29, 2015 (http://jointcenter.org/sites/default/files/Economic%20Burden%20of%20Health%20Inequalities%20Fact%20Sheet.pdf).

Lawless, Jennifer. 2004. "Politics of presence?: Congresswomen and Symbolic Representation." *Political Research Quarterly* 57(1):81–99.

Lawless, Jennifer. 2004. "Women, War, and Winning Elections: Gender Stereotyping in the Post September 11th Era." *Political Research Quarterly* 57(3):479–90.

Lawless, Jennifer and Richard Fox. 2012. *Men Rule: The Continued Under-Representation of Women in U.S. Politics.* Washington, DC: Women and Politics Institute at American University. Retrieved August 2015 (https://www.american.edu/spa/wpi/upload/2012-Men-Rule-Report-final-web.pdf).

Lee, Barbara. "Congresswoman Lee Marks Equal Pay Day, Calls for Renewed Effort to Ensure Equal Pay for Equal Work." *House.gov.* April 12, 2015 (https://lee.house.gov/news/press-releases/congresswoman-lee-marks-equal-pay-day-calls-for-renewed-effort-to-ensure-equal-pay-for-equal-work).

Levine, Bettijane., 1993. "Behind the 'Lani Guinier Mask': Months After Her Nomination Ordeal, She Says the Public Still Doesn't Know Who She Really Is." *Los Angeles Times,* December 7 (http://articles.latimes.com/1993–12–07/news/vw-64911_1_lani-guinier).

Lillie-Blanton, Marsha and Catherine Hoffman. 2005. "The Role of Health Insurance Coverage in Reducing Racial/Ethnic Disparities in Health Care." *Health Affairs* 24(2):398–408.

Lim, Chaeyoon. 2008. "Social Networks and Political Participation: How Do Networks Matter?" *Social Forces* 87(2):961–82.

Lovlace, Ryan. 2015. "How Republicans Hope To Turn Virginia Red in 2016." *The Washington Examiner,* July 6 (http://www.washingtonexaminer.com/how-republicans-hope-to-turn-virginia-red-in-2016/article/2567449).

Luo, Michael. 2008. "Small Online Contributions Add Up to Huge Fund-Raising Edge for Obama." *The New York Times,* February 20 (http://www.nytimes.com/2008/02/20/us/politics/20obama.html?_r=0).

MacDonald, Jason and Erin O'Brien. 2011. "Quasi-Experimental Design, Constituency, and Advancing Women's Interests: Reexamining the influence of gender on substantive representation." *Political Research Quarterly* 64(2):472–86.

MacManus, Susan. 2014. "Voter Participation and Turnout: The Political Generation Divide Among Women Voters." Pp. 80–118 in *Gender & Elections: Shaping the future of American politics,* edited by S. Carroll and R. Fox. New York, NY: Cambridge University Press.

Mansbridge, Jane. 1999. "Should Blacks Represent Blacks and Women Represent Women? A Contingent 'Yes.'" *Journal of Politics* 61(3):628–57.

Mann, Thomas and Raffaela Wakeman. 2013. *Voting Rights after Shelby County v. Holder.*Washington, DC: Brookings Institution. Retrieved June 12, 2015.

http://www.brookings.edu/blogs/up-front/posts/2013/06/25-supreme-court-voting-rights-act-mann-wakeman.

Maraniss, David and Susan Schmidt. 1996. "Hillary Clinton and the Whitewater Controversy: A Close-Up." *The Washington Post*, June 2 (https://www.washingtonpost.com/wp-srv/politics/special/whitewater/stories/wwtr960602.htm).

Margasak, Larry. "California Congresswoman Maxine Waters Charged with Ethics Violations. 2010." *CBS News*, August 2 (http://www.cbsnews.com/8301–503544_162–20012335-503544.html).

Mayer, Jane. 2016. *Dark Money: The Hidden History of the Billionaires behind the Rise of the Radical Right*. New York, NY: Random House.

Mears, Bill and Greg Botelho. June 2013. "'Outrageous' or overdue?: Court Strikes Down Part of Historic Voting Rights Law?" *Cable News Network*, June 6 (http://www.cnn.com/2013/06/25/politics/scotus-voting-rights/).

Merica, Dan. 2015. "Windfall at Bernie's: Sanders raises $1.5 million in 24 hours." *Cable News Network*, May 1 (http://www.cnn.com/2015/05/01/politics/bernie-sanders-fundraising/).

Miller, Jake. 2014. "GOP Presidential Race Looms as Large as Potential Hopefuls Gather." *CBS News*, March 29 (http://www.cbsnews.com/news/chris-christie-scott-walker-john-kasich-avoid-talk-of-2016-in-vegas/).

Miller, Sunlen. 2012. "Birth Control Hearing Was 'Like Stepping Into a Time Machine.'" *ABC News*, February 17 (http://abcnews.go.com/blogs/politics/2012/02/birth-control-hearing-was-like-stepping-into-a-time-machine/).

Milyo, Jeffrey and Samantha Schosberg. 2000. "Gender Bias and Selection Bias in House Elections." *Public Choice* 105(1/2):41–59.

Minta, Michael and Nadia Brown. 2014. "Gender, Race, and Congressional Attention to Women's Issues." *DuBois Review* 11(2):253–72.

Minta, Michael and Valeria Sinclair-Chapman. 2013. "Diversity in Political Institutions and Congressional Responsiveness to Minority Interests. *Political Research Quarterly* 66(1):127–40.

Moncrief, Gary and Joel Thompson. 1991. "Gender, Race, and the State Legislature: A Research Note on the Double Disadvantage Hypothesis." *Social Science Journal* 28(4):481–88.

Morris, Monique. 2009. *Discrimination and Mortgage Lending in America: A Summary of theDisparate Impact of Subprime Mortgage Lending on African Americans*. Baltimore, MD: National Association for the Advancement of Colored People. Retrieved November 22, 2015 (www.naacp.org).

Mosendz, Polly. 2015. "Dylann Roof Confesses: Says He Wanted to Start a 'Race War.'" *Newsweek*, June 19 (http://www.newsweek.com/dylann-roof-confesses-church-shooting-says-he-wanted-start-race-war-344797/).

Moss, Hillary. 2009. "Coat of Many colors? Love it or Lose it?" *Huffington Post*, May 25 (http://www.huffingtonpost.com/2009/09/28/hillary-clintons-coat-of_n_301976.html).

National Conference of State Legislatures. 2014. *Voter ID History*. Washington, DC: National Conference of State Legislatures. Retrieved July 11, 2015 (http://www.ncsl.org/research/elections-and-campaigns/voter-id-history.aspx).

National Public Radio. 2003. Former Senator Carol Moseley Braun. Washington, DC: National Public Radio. Retrieved January 12, 2015 (http://www.npr.org/programs/specials/democrats2004/transcripts/braun_trans.html).

Newport, Frank and Lydia Saad. 2008. *Black Men, Women Equally Likely to Support Obama: Gender Gap Evident Among Whites and Hispanics.* Washington, DC: Gallup Poll, Retrieved September 5, 2015 (http://www.gallup.com/poll/104275/Black-Men-Women-Equally-Likely-Support-Obama).

Nier III, Charles and Maureen St. Cyr. 2011. "A Racial Financial Crisis: Rethinking the Theory of Reverse Redlining to Combat Predatory Lending Under the Fair Housing Act." *Temple Law Review* 83:941–78.

Office of the White House Press Secretary. 2010. *Remarks by the President and Dr. Jill Biden at White House Summit on Community Colleges.* Washington, DC: White House. Retrieved November 12, 2015 (https://www.whitehouse.gov/the-press-office/2010/10/05/remarks-president-and-dr-jill-biden-white-house-summit-community-college).

Okpalaoka, Ugonna. 2012. "Obama's 2012 Campaign Tops Digital Fundraising in 2008." *The Grio,* November 16 (http://thegrio.com/2012/11/16/obamas-2012-campaign-tops-digital-fundraising-in-2008/).

Oliver, Mary B. 2003. "African-American Men as 'Criminal and Dangerous': Implications of Media Portrayals of Crime on the 'Criminalization' of African-American Men." *Journal of African-American Studies* 7(2):3–18.

O'Reilly, Kenneth. 1999. "Race and the Presidency." Pp. 1571–75 in *Africana: The Encyclopedia of the African and African American Experience,* edited by K. A. Appiah and H. L. Gates. New York, NY: Basic Civitas Books.

O'rey, Byron D'Andra', Wendy Smooth, Kimberly Adams, and Kisha Harris-Clark. 2006. "Race and Gender Matter: Refining Models of Legislative Policy Making in State Legislatures." *Journal of Women, Politics & Policy* 28(3/4):97–119.

Oxley, Zoe and Richard L. Fox. 2004. "Women in Executive Office: Variation across American States." *Political Research Quarterly* 57(1):113–20.

Pager, D. 2003. "The Mark of a Criminal Record." *American Journal of Sociology* 108(5):937–75.

Pappas, G., W. C. Hadden, L. J. Kozak, and G. F. Fisher. 1997. "Potentially Avoidable Hospitalizations: Inequities in Rates Between U.S. Socioeconomic Groups." *American Journal of Public Health* 87(5):811–17.

Parham-Payne, Wanda, Bette Dickerson, and Tekisha D. Everette. 2013. "Trading the Picket Fence: Perceptions of Childbirth, Marriage, and Career." *Journal of Sociology and Social Welfare* 40(3):85–105.

Parham-Payne, Wanda and Autumn Saxton-Ross. 2010. "Obama's Health Care Plan: The Perceptions of Professionals and the People." *Journal of Race and Policy* 6(1):62–79.

Patten, Eileen. 2015. How Millennials Today Compare with their Grandparents 50 Years Ago. Washington, DC: Pew Research Center. Retrieved November 19, 2015 (http://www.pewresearch.org/fact-tank/2015/03/19/how-millennials-compare-with-their-grandparents/).

Pearson, Kathryn. 2010. "Demographic Change and the Future of Congress." *PS: Political Science & Politics* 235–38.

Pearson, Kathryn and Logan Dancy. 2011. "Elevating Women's Voices in Congress: Speech Participation in the House of Representatives." *Political Research Quarterly* 64(4):910–23.

Peruche, B. M. and E. B. Plant. 2006. "The Correlates of Law Enforcement Officers' Automaticand Controlled Race-Based Responses to Criminal Suspects." *Basic and Applied Social Psychology* 28(2):193–99.

Pew Research Center. 2013. *Intermarriage on the Rise in the U.S.* Washington, DC: Pew Research Center. Retrieved June 15, 2015 (http://www.pewresearch.org/daily-number/intermarriage-on-the-rise-in-the-u-s/1111111).

Pew Research Center. 2015. 2014 Party Identification Detailed Tables. Washington, DC Pew Research Center. Retrieved December 11, 2015 (http://www.people-press.org/2015/04/07/2014-party-identification-detailed-tables-black-non-hispanic/).

Philpot, Tasha and Hanes Walton. 2007. "One of Our Own: Black Female Candidates and the Voters Who Support Them." *American Journal of Political Science* 51(1):49–62.

Pinney, Neil and George Serra. 2002. "A Voice for Black Interests: Congressional Black Caucus Cohesion and Bill Sponsorship." *Congress & the Presidency* 29(1):69–88.

Piston, Spencer. 2010. "How Explicit Racial Prejudice Hurt Obama in the 2008 Election." *Political Behavior* 32:431–51.

Poggione, Sarah. 2004. "Exploring Gender Differences in State Legislators' Policy Preferences." *Political Research Quarterly* 57(2):305–15.

Posavac, Heidi, Steven Posavac, and Emil Posavac. 1998. "Exposure to Media Images of Female Attractiveness and Concern with Body Weight among Young Women." *Sex Roles* 38(3/4):187–92.

Posavac, Heidi, Steven Posavac, and Richard Weigel. 2001. "Reducing the Impact of Media Images on Women at Risk for Body Image Disturbance: Three Targeted Interventions." *Journal of Social and Clinical Psychology* 20(3):324–40.

Post, Deborah. 2009. "Cultural Inversion and the One-Drop Rule: An Essay on Biology, Racial Classification, and the Rhetoric of Racial Transcendence." *Albany Law Review* 72(4):909–28.

Prestage, Jewel. 1991. "In Quest of African American Political Woman." *The Annals of the American Academy of Political and Social Science* 515:88–103.

Preuhs, Robert R. 2006. "The Conditional Effects of Minority Descriptive Representation: African-American Legislators and Policy Influence in the American States." *The Journal of Politics* 68:585–99.

Preuhs, Robert R. and Rodney Hero. 2011. "A Different Kind of Representation: Black and Latino Descriptive Representation and the Role of Ideological Cuing." *Political Research Quarterly* 64(1):157–71.

Puente, Maria. 2008. "What Kind of First Lady Will She Be?" *USA Today.* December 18 (http://www.usatoday.com/life/people/2008–12–18-michelleobama-firstlady_N.htm).

Robertson, Terry, Kristin Froemling, Scott Wells, and Shannon McCraw. 1999. "Sex, Lies, and Videotape: An Analysis of Gender in Campaign Advertisements." *Communication Quarterly* 47(3):333–41.

Robillard, Kevin. 2012. "GOP Chief: Mystery Black Voters" *Politico*, November 15 (http://www.politico.com/news/stories/1112/83895.html).

Robinson, Randall. 1999. *Defending the Spirit: A Black Life in America.* New, NY: Penguin Group.

Robnett, Belinda and James Bany. 2011. "Gender, Church Involvement and African-American Political Participation. *Sociological Perspectives* 54(4):689–712.

Rocca, Michael, Gabriel Sanchez, and Ron Nikora. 2009. "The Role of Personal Attributes in African American Roll-Call Voting Behavior in Congress." *Political Research Quarterly* 62(2):408–15.

Roman, John. 2013. *Race, Justifiable Homicide, and Stand Your Ground Laws: Analysis of FBI Supplementary Homicide Report Data.* Washington, DC: Urban Institute. Retrieved September 10, 2015 (https://www.ncjrs.gov/App/Publications/abstract.aspx?ID=265405).

Ross, Lawrence. 2001. *The Divine Nine: The History of African American Fraternities and Sororities.* New York, NY: Kensington Publishing.

Rousseau, Nicole. 2009. *Black Woman's Burden: Commidifying Black Reproduction.* New York, NY: Palgrave Macmillan.

Rucker, Philip. 2014. "Hillary Clinton on Iraq Vote: 'I Still Got It Wrong. Plain and Simple.'" *The Washington Post*, June 5 (http://www.washingtonpost.com/blogs/post-politics/wp/2014/06/05/hillary-clinton-on-iraq-vote-i-still-got-it-wrong-plain-and-simple/).

Rudin, Ken. 2003. *National Public Radio interview with Carol Moseley-Braun.* Washington, DC: National Public Radio. Retrieved May 3, 2015 (http://www.npr.org/programs/specials/democrats2004/braun.html).

Ruggeri, Amanda. 2009. Michelle Obama. *U.S. News and World Report.*

Sabato, Larry. 1985. *PAC Power: Inside the World of Political Action Committees.* New York, NY: W. W. Norton and Company.

Sakuma, Amanda. 2012. "Black Voters 'Deeply Offended' by Maine GOP chair." *MSNBC*, November 17 (http://www.msnbc.com/melissa-harris-perry/black-voters-deeply-offended-maine-gop-c).

Samuels, Allison. 2009. "How Will Michelle Obama Make Her Mark?" *Newsweek*, October 23 (http://www.newsweek.com/what-michelle-obama-must-do-now-81263).

Sanbonmatsu, Kira and Kathleen Dolan. 2009. "Do Gender Stereotypes Transcend Party?" *Political Research Quarterly* 62(3):485–94.

Savage, David. 2013. "Supreme Court Strikes Down Key Section of Voting Rights Act." *Los Angeles Times*, June 25 (http://articles.latimes.com/2013/jun/25/news/la-pn-supreme-court-voting-rights-ruling-20130625).

Schemo, Diane Jean. 2001. "Persistent Racial Segregation Mars Suburbs' Green Dream." in *Race, Class, and Gender in the United States. 5th Edition*, edited by P. S. Rothenberg. New York, NY: Worth Publishers.

Schlehofer, Michele, Bettina Casad, Michelle Bligh, and Angela Grotto. 2011. "Navigating Public Prejudices: The Impact of Media and Attitudes on High-Profile Female Political Leaders." *Sex Roles* 65:69–83.

Schwartzman, Paul. 2015. "Former D. C. Mayor Vincent C. Gray Eyeing Comeback, Associates Say," October 2 (https://www.washingtonpost.com/local/former-dc-mayor-vincent-c-gray-eyeing-comeback-associates-say/2015/10/01/553fdbc6-6888-11e5-8325-a42b5a459b1e_story.html).

Schwartzman, Paul and Hauslohner. 2016. "Vincent Gray Tests the Waters and Weighs a Return to D.C. Politics." *The Washington Post*, February 2 (https://www.

washingtonpost.com/local/vincent-gray-tests-the-waters-and-weighs-a-return-to-dc-politics/2016/02/02/9d2671fe-c6aa-11e5-a4aa-f25866ba0dc6_story.html).

Sebold, Karen, Scott Limbocker, Andrew Dowdle, and Patrick Stewart. 2012. "The Political Geography of Campaign Finance: Contributions to 2008 Republican Presidential Candidates." *PS: Political Science & Politics*:688–93.

Sewell, C. 2013. "Mammies and Matriarchs: Tracing the Images of the Black Female in Popular Culture 1950s to Present." *Journal of African American Studies* 17:308–26.

Siegel, Joel. 2011. "Clarence Thomas-Anita Hill Supreme Court Confirmation Hearing "Empowered Women' and Panel Member Arlen Specter Still Amazed by Reactions." *ABC News*, October 24 (http://abcnews.go.com/US/clarence-thomas-anita-hill-supreme-court-confirmation-hearing/story?id=14802217).

Simon, Richard. 2010. "Maxine Waters Accused of Three Ethics Violations." *Los Angeles Times*, August 10 (http://articles.latimes.com/2010/aug/10/nation/la-na-maxine-waters-20100810).

Sinclair-Chapman, Valeria, and Melanie Price. 2008. "Black Politics, the 2008 Election, and the (Im)Possibility of Race Transcendence." *PS: Political Science & Politics* 41(4):739–37.

Sklar, Kathleen Kish. 2008. "A Women's History Report Card on Hillary Rodham Clinton's Presidential Primary Campaign, 2008." *Feminist Studies* 34(1/2):315–47.

Smith, Eric R. A. N. and Richard Fox. 2001. "The Electoral Fortunes of Women Candidates for Congress." *Political Research Quarterly* 54(1):205–21.

Smith-Shomade, B. 2003. "Rock-a-Bye Baby!: Black Women Disrupting Gangs and Constructing Hip-Hop Gangsta Films." *Cinema Journal* 42(2):26–40.

Smooth, Wendy. 2006. "Intersectionality in Electoral Politics: A Mess Worth Making." *Politics & Gender* 2(3):400–14.

Smooth, Wendy. 2011. "Standing for Women? Which Women? The Substantive Representation of Women's Interests and the Research Imperative of Intersectionality." *Politics & Gender* 7(3):436–41.

Smooth, Wendy. 2014. "African American Women and Electoral Politics: Translating Voting Power into Office Holding." Pp. 167–89. in *Gender & Elections: Shaping the Future of American Politics*, edited by S. and R. Fox. New York, NY: Cambridge University Press.

Sokhey, Anand and Paul Djupe. 2011. "Interpersonal Networks and Democratic Politics." *PS: Political Science & Politics* 55–59.

Stolberg, Sheryl Gay. 2014. "In Georgia, Politics Move Past Just Black and White. *New York Times*, September 18 (http://www.nytimes.com/2014/09/19/us/politics/as-georgias-population-changes-its-politics-begin-to-follow.html).

Stone, Andrea. 2012. "Mitt Romney's 'Wawa' Gaffe Just Latest Out-of-Touch Politician Moment." *Huffington Post*, June 19 (http://www.huffingtonpost.com/2012/06/19/mitt-romney-wawa-gaffe-out-of-touch-politicians_n_1608648.html).

Strauss, Gary. 2002. "Good Old Boys' Network Still Rules Corporate Boards." *USA Today*. November 5 (http://usatoday30.usatoday.com/money/companies/management/2002-10-31-minority-report_x.htm).

Sullivan, Patricia. 1999. "Civil Rights Movement." Pp. 441–55 in *Africana: The Encyclopedia of the African and African American Experience*, edited by K. A. Appiah and H. L. Gates. New York, NY: Basic Civitas Books.

Suro, Roberto. 1991. "The Thomas Nomination; A Law Professor Defends Integrity" *The New York Times*, October 8 (http://www.nytimes.com/1991/10/08/us/the-thomas-nomination-a-law-professor-defends-integrity.html).

Swers, Michele. 2001. "Understanding the Policy Impact of Electing Women: Evidence from Research on Congress and State Legislatures." *PS: Political Science & Politics* 34(2):217–20.

Tam, Ruth. 2014. "Carol Moseley Braun: 'Small Wonder' There Is Not More Diversity in Congress". *The Washington Post*, February 26 (http://www.washingtonpost.com/blogs/she-the-people/wp/2014/02/26/carol-moseley-braun-small-wonder-there-is-not-more-diversity-in-congress/).

Tate, Katherine. 1999. "Blacks in American Electoral Politics. Pp. 79–81 in *Africana: The Encyclopedia of the African and African American Experience*, edited by K. A. Appiah and H. L. Gates. New York, NY: Basic Civitas Books.

Taylor, Paul, and Mark Hugo Lopez. 2013. *Six Take-Aways from the Census Bureau's Voting Report*. Washington, DC: Pew Research Center. Retrieved June 19, 2015 (http://www.pewresearch.org/fact-tank/2013/05/08/six-take-aways-from-the-census-bureaus-voting-report/).

Taylor, Paul, Rich Morin, Eileen Patten, and D' Vera Cohn. 2012. *Fewer, Poorer, Gloomier: The Lost Decade of the Middle Class*. Washington, DC: Pew Research Center. Retrieved July 6, 2015 (http://www.pewsocialtrends.org/files/2012/08/pew-social-trends-lost-decade-of-the-middle-class.pdf).

Taylor, Steven. 2011. "Racial Polarization in the 2008 U.S. Presidential Election." *The Western Journal of Black Studies* 35(2):118–27.

Terrell, Mary Church. 2005. *A Colored Woman in a White World*. Amherst, NY: Humanity Books.

Thomas, Sue. 1997. "Why Gender Matters: The Perceptions of Women Officeholders." *Women & Politics* 17(1):27–42.

Thomas, Sue. 2002. "The Personal is the Political: Antecedents of Gendered Choices of Elected Representatives." *Sex Roles* 47(7/8):343–54.

Tien, Charles and Dena Levy. 2008. "The Influence of African Americans on Congress: A Content Analysis of the Civil Rights Debate." *Du Bois Review* 5(1):115–315.

Tolbert, C. and G. Steuernagel. 2009. "Women Lawmakers, State Mandates, and Women's Health." *Women and Politics* 22(2):1–39.

Truth, Sojourner. 1997. *The Narrative of Sojourner Truth*. New York, NY: Dover Publications.

Tuck, Stephen. 2007. "Democratization and the Disfranchisement of African Americans in the U.S. South during the Late 19th Century." *Democratization* 14(4):580–602.

United States Census Bureau. 2000. *Profiles of General Demographic Characteristics: 2000 Census of Population and Housing Characteristics*. Suitland, MD: United States Census Bureau. Retrieved May 10, 2015 (https://www.census.gov/prod/cen2000/dp1/2kh00.pdf).

United States Census Bureau. 2010. *Profile of General Population and Housing Characteristics: 2010.* Suitland, MD: United States Census Bureau. Retrieved May 10, 2015 (https://www.census.gov/history/pdf/2010angelscamp.pdf).

United States Census Bureau. 2012. *Most Children Younger than Age 1 are Minorities.* Suitland, MD: United States Census Bureau. Retrieved June 6, 2015 (https://www.census.gov/newsroom/releases/archives/population/cb12–90.html).

U.S. Census Bureau. 2013. *The Diversifying Electorate: Voting Rates by Race and Hispanic Origin in 2012 (And Other Recent Elections).* Suitland, MD: United States Census Bureau. Retrieved May 11, 2015 (https://www.census.gov/prod/2013pubs/p20–568.pdf).

United States Census Bureau. 2014. *American Finder: Prince William County, Virginia.* Suitland, MD: United Census Bureau. Retrieved June 5, 2015 (http://factfinder.census.gov/faces/tableservices/jsf/pages/productview.xhtml?src=bkmk).

United States Census Bureau. 2014. *Fast Facts for Congress.* Suitland, MD: United States Census Bureau. Retrieved January 26, 2016 (http://www.census.gov/fastfacts/).

United States Census Bureau. 2015. *State and County Quick Facts.* Suitland, MD: United States Census Bureau, Retrieved May 15, 2015 (http://quickfacts.census.gov/qfd/states/00000.html).

U.S. Department of Education. 2014. *The Condition of Education, 2014.* Washington, DC: National Center for Education Statistics. Retrieved April 26, 2015 (http://nces.ed.gov/pubs2014/2014083.pdf).

Vargas, Antonio. 2008. "Obama Raised Half a Billion Online." *The Washington Post,* November 20 (http://voices.washingtonpost.com/44/2008/11/obama-raised-half-a-billion-on.html).

Volden, Craig, Alan Wiseman, and Dana Wittmer. 2010. "Women's Issues and Their Fates in Congress. Center for the Study of Democratic Institutions." Working Paper.

Vozzella, Laura. 2014. "As Virginia's Demographics Have Changed, So Has Mark Warner's Campaign Approach." *The Washington Post,* August 7 (https://www.washingtonpost.com/local/virginia-politics/as-virginias-demographics-have-changed-so-has-mark-warners-campaign-approach/2014/08/07/29902c22–1115–11e4–9285–4243a40ddc97_story.html).

Wallace, David, Amryn Abduq-Khaliq, Michael Czuchry, Tiffany Sia. 2009. "African-American's Political Attitudes, Party Affiliation, and Voting Behavior." *Journal of African American Studies* 13(2):139–46.

Walters, Ronald. 2008. "Obama's Edge: Understanding Nation Time." *The Black Scholar* 38(1):24–33.

Walton, Hanes Jr. 2001. "The Disenfranchisement of the African American Voter in the 2000 Presidential Election: The Silence of the Winner and Loser." *The Black Scholar* 31(2):21–24.

Ward, T. and P. Ong. 2006. "Race and Space: Hiring Practices of Los Angeles Electronic Firms." *Journal of Urban Affairs* 28(5):511–26.

Waters, Maxine (CA). (20 May 2015). "Transportation Infrastructure." *Congressional Record* 161(78):H3496–H3501.

Weaver, Vesla. 2012. "The Electoral Consequences of Skin Color: The 'Hidden' Side of Race in Politics." *Political Behavior* 34:159–92.

Weinberger, Oddone, and Henderson. 1996. "Does Increased Access to Primary Care Reduce Hospital Admissions?" *New England Journal of Medicine* 334(22):1441–47.

Weiser, Wendy and Erick Opsal. 2014. *The State of Voting in 2014*. New York. NY: Brennan Center for Justice at the New York University School of Law. Retrieved April 30, 2015 (http://www.brennancenter.org/sites/default/files/analysis/State_of_Voting_2014.pdf).

Wheaton, Sarah. 2007. "Latest Campaign Issue? One Candidate's Neckline." *The New York Times*, July 28 (http://www.nytimes.com/2007/07/28/us/politics/28hillary.html?_r=0).

Willis, Derek. "In a Short Time, Ted Cruz Has Raised Big Money From Small Donors." *The New York Times*, April 2 (http://www.nytimes.com/2015/04/03/upshot/what-ted-cruzs-early-fund-raising-means-and-doesnt.html).

Wise, Tim. 2009. *Between Barack and a Hard Place: Racism and White Denial in the Age of Obama*. San Francisco, CA: City Lights Books.

Witt, Linda, Karen Paget, and Glenna Matthews. 1995. *Running As a Woman: Gender and Power in American Politics*. New York, NY: Free Press.

Wotzencraft, Ann. 2001. "Gender Bias on Wall Street." in *Race, Class, and Gender in the United States, 5th Edition*, edited by P. S. Rothenberg. New York, NY: Worth Publishers.

Zornick, George. 2012. "Republican Hearing on Contraception: No Women Allowed." *The Nation*, February 16 (http://www.thenation.com/article/republican-hearing-contraception-no-women-allowed/).

Zuvekas, Samuel and George Taliaferro. 2003. "Pathways to Access: Health Insurance, the Health Care Delivery System, and Racial/Ethnic Disparities, 1996–1999." *Health Affairs* 22(2):139–53.

Index

About the Author

As a social scientist for approximately 16 years, the author, **Dr. Wanda V. Parham-Payne**, initially began her career as a research consultant conducting formative and summative evaluations of federally funded programs and initiatives. During her time as an applied researcher, she crafted research designs and employed various research methodologies including focus groups (face to face and online), participant observations, semi-structured interviews, telephone interviews, paper-and-pencil surveys, and computer-assisted surveys. Subsequent to her employment as a consultant, Dr. Parham-Payne worked as an analyst for the District of Columbia's Department of Health Care Finance (DHCF). Currently, Dr. Parham-Payne serves as an Assistant Professor of Sociology and the Sociology Program Coordinator within the Department of Psychological and Sociological Sciences at Prince George's Community College in Largo, Maryland. She is also an Adjunct Professorial Lecturer of Sociology at American University in Washington, DC. Her research interests primarily include the intersection of race, gender, and class; African-American women in the political arena; cultural competence in healthcare/minority health disparities; and the African-American family. Dr. Parham-Payne's research has been published in *Advances in Gender Research*, *Journal of African American Studies*, *Journal of Black Studies*, *Journal of Race and Policy*, and the *Journal of Sociology and Social Welfare*. She holds a bachelor of arts in political science from Elizabeth City State University. Dr. Parham-Payne also has a master's degree in public administration from Old Dominion University and a doctor of philosophy in sociology from Howard University.

Lightning Source UK Ltd.
Milton Keynes UK
UKOW04n1022291117

313541UK00007B/191/P